An Analysis of

Niccolò Machiavelli's

The Prince

Ben Worthy
with
Riley Quinn

www.macat.com
info@macat.com

Cover illustration: Capucine Deslouis

Cataloguing in Publication Data
A catalogue record for this book is available from the British Library.
Library of Congress Cataloguing-in-Publication Data is available upon request.

ISBN 978-1-912303-36-6 (hardback)
ISBN 978-1-912127-61-0 (paperback)
ISBN 978-1-912282-24-1 (e-book)

Notice

CONTENTS

THE MACAT LIBRARY

The Macat Library is a series of unique academic explorations of seminal works in the humanities and social sciences – books and papers that have had a significant and widely recognised impact on their disciplines. It has been created to serve as much more than just a summary of what lies between the covers of a great book. It illuminates and explores the influences on, ideas of, and impact of that book. Our goal is to offer a learning resource that encourages critical thinking and fosters a better, deeper understanding of important ideas.

Each publication is divided into three Sections: Influences, Ideas, and Impact. Each Section has four Modules. These explore every important facet of the work, and the responses to it.

This Section-Module structure makes a Macat Library book easy to use, but it has another important feature. Because each Macat book is written to the same format, it is possible (and encouraged!) to cross-reference multiple Macat books along the same lines of inquiry or research. This allows the reader to open up interesting interdisciplinary pathways.

To further aid your reading, lists of glossary terms and people mentioned are included at the end of this book (these are indicated by an asterisk [*] throughout) – as well as a list of works cited.

Macat has worked with the University of Cambridge to identify the elements of critical thinking and understand the ways in which six different skills combine to enable effective thinking.
Three allow us to fully understand a problem; three more give us the tools to solve it. Together, these six skills make up the **PACIER** model of critical thinking. They are:

ANALYSIS – understanding how an argument is built
EVALUATION – exploring the strengths and weaknesses of an argument
INTERPRETATION – understanding issues of meaning

CREATIVE THINKING – coming up with new ideas and fresh connections
PROBLEM-SOLVING – producing strong solutions
REASONING – creating strong arguments

To find out more, visit **WWW.MACAT.COM.**

CRITICAL THINKING AND *THE PRINCE*

Primary critical thinking skill: INTERPRETATION
Secondary critical thinking skill: CREATIVE THINKING

How should rulers rule? What is the nature of power? These questions had already been asked when Niccolò Machiavelli wrote *The Prince* in 1513. But what made his thinking on the topic different was his ability to interpret evidence: to look at old issues and find new meaning within them.

Many of Machiavelli's contemporaries thought that God would make sure morality was rewarded. To these people, it was inevitable that ethical individuals would enjoy success in this world and attain paradise in the next. Machiavelli was not so sure. He used the evidence of history to prove that people who can lie, cheat and murder tend to succeed.

Machiavelli concluded that three main factors affect a political leader's success or failure. In doing so, he reached an entirely new understanding of the meaning of his evidence. Machiavelli argued that behaving in a moral way actually hinders a ruler. If everyone acted morally, he reasoned, then morals would not be a disadvantage. But in a world in which leaders are willing to be ruthless, a moral leader would make both themselves and their state vulnerable. Machiavelli's novel interpretation posits that morals can make a leader hesitate, and this could cost them – and the citizens they are responsible for – everything.

ABOUT THE AUTHOR OF THE ORIGINAL WORK

Niccolò Machiavelli was born in 1469, in the Italian city-state of Florence. When he was in his twenties, Florence became a republic and Machiavelli one of its important civil servants. But 19 years on, former ruling family, the Medicis, defeated the republican government and returned to power. Machiavelli was imprisoned, tortured, and then exiled. His experiences—both of wielding power and having it wielded against him—influenced the ideas he laid out in his world-famous book, *The Prince*.

ABOUT THE AUTHORS OF THE ANALYSIS

Dr Ben Worthy is Lecturer in Politics at Birkbeck, University of London. His research interests include government transparency, open data and political leadership, and he is the author of *The Politics of Freedom of Information: How and Why Governments Pass Laws That Threaten Their Power.*

Riley Quinn holds master's degrees in politics and international relations from both LSE and the University of Oxford.

ABOUT MACAT

GREAT WORKS FOR CRITICAL THINKING

Macat is focused on making the ideas of the world's great thinkers accessible and comprehensible to everybody, everywhere, in ways that promote the development of enhanced critical thinking skills.

It works with leading academics from the world's top universities to produce new analyses that focus on the ideas and the impact of the most influential works ever written across a wide variety of academic disciplines. Each of the works that sit at the heart of its growing library is an enduring example of great thinking. But by setting them in context – and looking at the influences that shaped their authors, as well as the responses they provoked – Macat encourages readers to look at these classics and game-changers with fresh eyes. Readers learn to think, engage and challenge their ideas, rather than simply accepting them.

'Macat offers an amazing first-of-its-kind tool for interdisciplinary learning and research. Its focus on works that transformed their disciplines and its rigorous approach, drawing on the world's leading experts and educational institutions, opens up a world-class education to anyone.'

Andreas Schleicher,
Director for Education and Skills, Organisation for Economic
Co-operation and Development

'Macat is taking on some of the major challenges in university education ... They have drawn together a strong team of active academics who are producing teaching materials that are novel in the breadth of their approach.'

Prof Lord Broers,
former Vice-Chancellor of the University of Cambridge

'The Macat vision is exceptionally exciting. It focuses upon new modes of learning which analyse and explain seminal texts which have profoundly influenced world thinking and so social and economic development. It promotes the kind of critical thinking which is essential for any society and economy.
This is the learning of the future.'

Rt Hon Charles Clarke, former UK Secretary of State for Education

'The Macat analyses provide immediate access to the critical conversation surrounding the books that have shaped their respective discipline, which will make them an invaluable resource to all of those, students and teachers, working in the field.'

Professor William Tronzo, University of California at San Diego

WAYS IN TO THE TEXT

KEY POINTS

- Niccolò Machiavelli (1469–1527) was an Italian statesman and political thinker.
- *The Prince* says a political leader ought to be concerned only with what "really is" as opposed to what is moral.*
- *The Prince* was the first book to expose the hypocrisy of leaders who claim to be acting morally when in fact they are not.

Who was Niccolò Machiavelli?

Born in 1469, Niccolò Machiavelli was a statesman and thinker from the city-state of Florence, now part of Italy. When Machiavelli was young, the city was dominated by a rich family: the Medicis.* But in 1494 the Medicis lost their hold on power. For the next 19 years, the city was governed as a republic.

Machiavelli was 25 and working as a civil servant employed by the Florentine government when this happened. At the age of 29, he was made head of the second chancery, giving him responsibility for overseeing foreign affairs in the territories that Florence controlled. It was an important role, because the republic was threatened both by other city-states and by aggressive European powers like France.

The Medicis regained power in Florence in 1512, but the following year Machiavelli was accused of plotting to overthrow their regime and was imprisoned and tortured.[1] Exiled to the countryside and banned from political life, Machiavelli responded by writing *The Prince*. This book explored what rulers had to do to retain their power.

In his role as a civil servant Machiavelli had helped plan wars, but he was no general or leader. He studied historical accounts of the behavior of successful rulers to draw most of his conclusions in *The Prince*. Machiavelli's biographer, the American journalist and historian Miles Unger,* calls him a "mild-mannered scholar" and very different from his subject, the "bloodthirsty tyrant" of *The Prince*.

History, however, does not remember Machiavelli as a mild-mannered scholar. His ideas about power—and what rulers need to do to retain it—led to him being caricatured as a devil. His ideas have had a huge impact and are still debated today.

What Does *The Prince* Say?

In *The Prince*—written in 1513—Machiavelli discusses the relationship between morality* and politics. Basing his discussion on historical and contemporary political leaders, he asks probing questions. How should rulers rule? What is the nature of power? Will a prince who is generous, trusting and honest actually manage to take power?

Many of Machiavelli's contemporaries thought God would make sure morality was rewarded. Ethical princes would have both success in this world and paradise in the next. Machiavelli is not so sure. He uses the evidence of history to prove that princes who can lie, cheat and murder have a tendency to succeed.

From his study of the evidence Machiavelli concludes that three main factors affect the success or otherwise of a political leader:

The first is *virtù*.* A ruler who possesses *virtù* is skillful and intelligent, willing to dominate others and willing to pursue power.

The second is *necessita*:* being willing to do what is necessary, regardless of whether or not it is evil. The difference between these two qualities is that the man displaying *virtù* will kill his enemies without hesitation before they *become* enemies. The man displaying *necessita* will kill his enemies without hesitation *after* they become enemies.

The third factor is *fortuna*.* *Fortuna* is the power of luck. "Fortune," Machiavelli argues, "is a woman," and if you want to keep her under control it is necessary to beat her.[2] *Fortuna*, in other words, is the whim of fate. Unless *fortuna* is controlled with *virtù*, she will be the downfall of any prince who relies on her. Machiavelli believed that politics was the realm of action, not the realm of morals. Political fortune favors those who act proactively and decisively to advance themselves.

Machiavelli argues that morality, or behaving in a moral way, hinders a ruler. If everyone acted morally, morals would not be a disadvantage. But in a world where people are willing to be ruthless, a moral prince would make himself, and his state, vulnerable. His morals might make him hesitate to act—and this could cost him everything.

Yet Machiavelli does not say that princes should forget morality completely. Instead, he argues that successful princes should *pretend to be moral*. This increases their power. Society expects princes to be ethical, so a prince who is perceived as moral has greater authority. In other words, claiming to be moral is a necessary hypocrisy.

However, *The Prince* is much more than a set of instructions for would-be rulers. Although many people regarded Machiavelli as a teacher of tyrants, other people see him as one of the first champions of liberty. Alberico Gentili,* a sixteenth-century professor of civil law at the University of Oxford said, "His intention was not to instruct the tyrant," but rather to make "all his secrets clear."[3]

Gentili argued that Machiavelli exposed the hypocrisy of the powerful. He showed that the tyrant who says he is a saint is merely sweetening his tyranny. Machiavelli did not invent lying, nor was he the first to tell rulers to lie. He was the first to make it obvious that ruling a principality and being a good person were two very different things.

11

Why Does *The Prince* Matter?

"Anyone who picks up Machiavelli's *The Prince*," writes the American academic Harvey Mansfield,* "holds in his hands the most famous book on politics ever written."[4] This is not because of the advice Machiavelli gives to princes—which in some ways is obvious—it is because Machiavelli is exposing the *truth* of politics. He was one of the first authors to lay bare the hypocritical way in which tyrants claim to act on moral grounds.

Before *The Prince*, political writing nearly always began by imagining the higher, moral purpose of political society. "What," writers asked, "is the ideal society?" After *The Prince*, political thinking became far more realistic. Theorists started to consider what really happens in politics, rather than dreaming of moral perfection.

The seventeenth-century English philosophers Thomas Hobbes* and John Locke,* and the eighteenth-century Genevan philosopher Jean-Jacques Rousseau,* considered themselves scientists, rather than moral thinkers. They started from first principles—a theory of what humanity is really like. Then they imagined how and why selfish, animalistic, brutish humanity would rationally enter into a society. They concluded that humans would not create a society for moral reasons. They would create societies because it benefitted them to do so. Old political theorizing said mankind and human society had a moral purpose. Post-Machiavellian political theorizing said society exists to serve the needs of man. This idea—that society exists to serve the needs of man—is at the root of liberalism.* Machiavelli was among the first to introduce the concept.

The Prince contains two different messages. Machiavelli's message for the prince is that to retain power, power must be the only objective. The message for everyone else is that political power and morality are unconnected. We should beware those politicians who claim their justifications from God or virtue.

Reading *The Prince* will help people become keener participants in the political process. When politicians claim moral authority, Machiavelli prompts the question, "Why is this being claimed? What does this politician stand to gain?" *The Prince* casts a cynical light on politics: but this harsh light may well be justified.

KEY QUESTIONS

Synthesize: What is the difference between *virtù*, *necessita*, and *fortuna*?

Analyze: Which of these three is the most important and why?

Apply: Where do you draw the line between the ethical and the political? Why?

NOTES
1   Miles Unger, *Machiavelli: A Biography* (New York: Simon and Schuster, 2011), 1.

2   Niccolò Machiavelli, *The Prince* (Oxford: Oxford University Press, 2005), 87.

3   Alberico Gentili, quoted in Harvey C. Mansfield, introduction to *The Prince* by Niccolò Machiavelli (Chicago: University of Chicago Press, 1998), xix.

4   Mansfield, introduction, vii.

SECTION 1
INFLUENCES

MODULE 1
THE AUTHOR AND THE
HISTORICAL CONTEXT

KEY POINTS

* *The Prince* remains one of the most important works in politics. This is because of the distinction Machiavelli draws between morality* and political action.

* Machiavelli learned about politics as a minister in Florence. The city-state, part of modern-day Italy, was engaged in a number of conflicts during Machiavelli's lifetime.

* Machiavelli wrote *The Prince* during the Renaissance,* the period in the fifteenth and sixteenth century when there was rapid modernization in Europe.

Why Read this Text?

Niccolò Machiavelli's *The Prince* remains one of the most famous and controversial works on politics ever written. Written in 1513, when Machiavelli was 44, it was an essay on the nature of power—what separates effective statesmen from ineffective statesmen? Its core question is: what, if anything, is the relationship between morality and reality? This question remains central to the practice of politics. In 2013 the American sociologist Jared Diamond* told the *New York Times* newspaper that if there was one book the American president should read, it was *The Prince*. "Machiavelli is a crystal-clear realist who understands the limits and uses of power."[1]

Importantly, *The Prince* does not advance a theory of its own about the practice of power. Instead, it sets out principles of political leadership. *The Prince* exposes the hypocrisy underlying power politics. Leaders may claim the moral right to rule, but this is only one of many

> **❝** Wishing, therefore, to offer myself to Your Magnificence with some evidence of my devotion to you, I have not found among my belongings anything that I might value more or prize so much as the knowledge of the deeds of great men that I have learned from a long experience in modern affairs and a continuous study of antiquity. **❞**
>
> Machiavelli, *The Prince*

strategies they use to support their power. Machiavelli's unflinching realism was not taken well. He was seen as a kind of devil until as recently as the nineteenth century. This was not just because of the responses of his critics. Machiavelli's reputation was also affected by the people who admired him. Napoleon Bonaparte,* Benito Mussolini,* and Vladimir Lenin* were among the most vocal supporters of *The Prince* and "[Adolf] Hitler* kept a copy by his bedside."[2]

Author's Life

Machiavelli was born in 1469 and lived and worked in Renaissance Italy. He was a civil servant in the powerful city-state of his native Florence and was an active participant in the political process. "I have set down all that I know and have learnt," he wrote, "from a long experience of, and from constantly reading about, political affairs."[3] But he was no prince himself and certainly had no firsthand experience of actually leading conquering armies. The American historian Miles Unger,* in his biography of Machiavelli, noted that Machiavelli's prince of the book and Machiavelli himself "are something of an odd couple." There was a big difference between the prince, "the bloodthirsty tyrant, pitiless in the pursuit of power, ruthless, and cruel, and the mild-mannered scholar [Machiavelli] in his threadbare robe and slippers."[4]

Nonetheless, as a diplomat, Machiavelli was involved in delicate negotiations on behalf of Florence with other city-states. He would have met many important political figures of his time, including Louis XII,* the King of France, successive popes, and the ruthless Italian nobleman Cesare Borgia.* Before his death in 1507, Borgia, the illegitimate son of a pope, had set out to conquer a number of Italian cities and create his own kingdom. Machiavelli was to base much of *The Prince* on Borgia's actions. "I shall never," he wrote, "hesitate to cite Cesare Borgia and his actions."[5]

In 1513, at the age of 44, Machiavelli's fortunes declined. The Medici family,* who had previously dominated Florentine politics between 1434 and 1494, returned to power. Machiavelli was accused of conspiracy against the Medicis and was tortured, though he was later released.[6] As a result of his experiences Machiavelli had a deep understanding of power. He had seen the inner workings of politics at a level of firsthand detail not accessible to the vast majority of people. He understood how power is used by others. But he also understood what power looks like to the powerless.

Author's Background

Machiavelli lived during the Renaissance, a period that began in the fifteenth century in Italy and continued through the sixteenth century. Renaissance means "rebirth" and the term refers to a rediscovery of knowledge the ancient Greeks and Romans had, which had been forgotten in the medieval period.* Renaissance thought was considered rebellious—"a reaction against the culture, institutions, and principles of the Middle Ages," which were unscientific and traditional.[7] The Canadian historian Kenneth Bartlett* also notes that Renaissance scholars "described their world as something new, something special, something dramatically different from what had preceded it."[8] It was a period of development that saw the growth of humanism* and the advent of science.

The American academic Harvey Mansfield* suggested Machiavelli intended to create a "science" of politics. "Machiavelli," Mansfield says, argues that politicians "should align [their] values with facts in the sense of deeds."[9] By this he means that politicians should always act according to practical necessity rather than to an unscientific code of ethics.

The instability of Renaissance Italy may have gone a long way towards inspiring Machiavelli's "scientific" realism. He'd seen power in Florence pass from the hands of the Medici family to a radical priest named Savonarola* and then to a republican government—the Republic of Florence*—from 1502 to 1512. Machiavelli was a firm supporter of the Republic, but saw its overly ethical politics as the source of its downfall. According to Italian historian Maurizio Viroli,* the ruler of the Republic of Florence, Piero Soderini,* "under whom Machiavelli served as secretary, fell from power because he was unable to defend the republic effectively because of his commitment to honesty."[10] This "honesty" prevented him from using necessarily brutal and underhanded methods of safeguarding the Republic "against supporters of the Medici."[11] The Medici then returned to power and Machiavelli dedicated *The Prince* to the head of the family, Lorenzo di Piero de' Medici, as an attempt to ingratiate himself with the new political order.

NOTES

1   Jared Diamond, "Jared Diamond: By the Book," *New York Times*, January 17, 2013, accessed December 14, 2014, http://www.nytimes.com/2013/01/20/books/review/jared-diamond-by-the-book.html?pagewanted=all.

2   Michael Arditti, "Machiavelli's Dangerous Book for Men," *Telegraph*, January 19, 2008, accessed December 12, 2014, http://www.telegraph.co.uk/culture/books/non_fictionreviews/3670598/Machiavellis-dangerous-book-for-men.html, accessed 8/12/2014.

3   Miles Unger, *Machiavelli: A Biography* (New York: Simon and Schuster, 2011), 71.

4   Unger, *Machiavelli*, 9.

5   Niccolò Machiavelli, *The Prince* (Oxford: Oxford University Press, 2005), 48.

6   Quentin Skinner, *Machiavelli* (Oxford: Oxford University Press, 1981), 22.

7   Kenneth Bartlett, introduction to *The Civilization of the Italian Renaissance: A Sourcebook*, ed. Kenneth Bartlett (Toronto: University of Toronto Press, 2011), 1.

8   Bartlett, introduction, 1.

9   Harvey C. Mansfield, "Machiavelli's Political Science," *The American Political Science Review* 75, no. 2 (1981): 293.

10 Maurizio Viroli, introduction to *The Prince* by Niccolò Machiavelli (Oxford: Oxford University Press, 2005), xxxvii.

11 Viroli, introduction, xxxvii.

MODULE 2
ACADEMIC CONTEXT

KEY POINTS

- The study of politics is concerned with understanding the very nature of power; what it is and how it ought to be used.
- Ancient Greek thinkers enjoyed the intellectual pursuit of trying to work out how politics could and should work to benefit people.
- Machiavelli preferred the Romans' more realistic, problem-solving approach to politics.

The Work In Its Context

Political philosophy, according to the German American historian and political theorist Leo Strauss,* is driven by the question: "Are political things natural?"[1] This question is extremely important and has a number of implications. Are laws natural? If they are not natural, why should they be obeyed? Are different social classes divided by nature, or by convention (simply the way things have usually been done)? What is the basis of this division?

These questions are important because they go back to the Greek philosopher Aristotle* and his belief that "man is a political animal."[2] By this, Aristotle meant that man will always live in communities, so humans will always act in association with one another. The problems of politics—"how to preserve order, to protect the weak from the strong," and even "the overall goals communities should pursue"—are eternal.[3] Investigating these issues has been a consistent feature throughout most of recorded human history. Political philosophy aims to uncover the "nature" and "purpose" of "human association."[4]

> **❝** But of all motives, none is better adapted to secure influence and hold it fast than love; nothing is more foreign to that end than fear. **❞**
>
> Marcus Tullius Cicero, *De Officis*

"Nature" means the underlying forces that drive politics. "Purpose" means the ultimate aim of political action. Niccolò Machiavelli's *The Prince* is important because it provides a bridge between political philosophy—where the thinker's duty is to reflect on ideas about politics—and political science, which is analyzing the evidence to draw conclusions about politics.

Overview of the Field

The earliest political thinkers are commonly thought to be Greek, beginning with Socrates,* then Plato,* and then Aristotle. Socrates "did not develop a theory of political constitutions or a model of an ideal state; his goal was to obtain knowledge of the human good" and to derive rationally "the values that determine how we ought to live our lives."[5] Plato took this concern one step further in his famous work, *The Republic*. This was written as an imaginary conversation between Socrates and a number of other characters. Using Socrates as a mouthpiece, Plato lays out an ideal constitution for an imaginary city-state. His argument proceeds entirely from his imagination to fulfill its real goal: "an argument for individual justice."[6] Plato wrote that the aim of rule in a city ought to be that of "harmoniously uniting citizens by persuasion and necessity, causing them to share with each other the benefit each is capable of providing to the community at large."[7]

Plato is slightly more practical than Socrates, and Aristotle is slightly more practical than Plato. Aristotle explores which ways of governing city-states are the most materially advantageous. However, like Plato, Aristotle sees politics as existing "for the sake of mere life." By this he means for the mutual defense and advantage people can enjoy from living in political community. He continues, "… but it exists for the sake of the good life."[8] By this, Aristotle means that politics leads to the spiritual fulfillment that comes from living in a community. For all these classical thinkers, politics exists for the benefit of those involved in it. Engagement with a good public life does not lead to some other goal: it is an end in itself.

Academic Influences

Machiavelli was a devoted student of classical* history and philosophy but he was a vocal critic of the "old-fashioned" approaches of the Ancient Greeks and their tendency to "[dream] up republics and principalities which have never in truth been known to exist."[9] He preferred the Romans' realistic approach to politics. Romulus,* the founder of Rome and hero of the Roman historian Titus Livy's* work, was willing to be deceitful to preserve his state. When the future of Rome was threatened by a catastrophe—namely the lack of women in the city—he held a festival and invited all the neighboring tribes. "The Roman men," Livy explains, "[seized] the unmarried girls" of their neighbors, "violating their sacred obligations as hosts … contrary to religion and good faith."[10] Moreover, when this caused war between Rome and its neighbors, Romulus's skill in battle led him to victory. He "returned in triumph with his army, and, being an extraordinary man in his ability to publicize his achievements no less than in his execution of them,"[11] made a great show of strength in protecting his state's interests over any other considerations.

According to the Italian academic Maurizio Viroli,* Machiavelli loved Roman historians more than Roman political thinkers. Yet he was critical of the Roman jurist, orator, and politician Cicero.* Cicero said, "of all the motives, none is better adapted to secure influence and hold it fast than love; nothing is more foreign to that end than fear."[12]

Implicitly responding to Cicero, Machiavelli argues, "It is much safer to be feared than to be loved," and makes no mention of the ethics surrounding this decision.[13] For Machiavelli, ethics and politics were not the same thing.

NOTES

1   Leo Strauss, introduction to *History of Political Philosophy*, ed. Leo Strauss and Joseph Cropsey (Chicago: University of Chicago Press, 1987), 3.

2   Aristotle, quoted in George Klosko, *History of Political Theory: An Introduction: Volume II: Modern* (Oxford: Oxford University Press, 2013), 1.

3   Klosko, *History of Political Theory*, 1.

4   Klosko, *History of Political Theory*, 1.

5   Daniel Devereaux, "Classical Political Philosophy: Plato and Aristotle," in *The Oxford Handbook of the History of Political Philosophy*, ed. George Klosko (Oxford: Oxford University Press, 2011), 98.

6   Devereaux, "Classical Political Philosophy," 101.

7   Plato, *The Republic*, trans. R. E. Allen (New Haven: Yale University Press, 2006), 234.

8   Thomas L. Pangle and Timothy W. Burns, *The Key Texts of Political Philosophy: An Introduction* (Cambridge: University of Cambridge Press, 2015), 89.

9   Niccolò Machiavelli, *The Prince* (London: Penguin Books, 2003), 50.

10   Livy, *The Rise of Rome: Books 1–5*, trans. T. J. Luce (Oxford: Oxford University Press, 1998), 14.

11   Livy, *Rise*, 15.

12   Cicero, quoted in Maruizio Viroli, introduction to *The Prince* by Niccolò Machiavelli (Oxford: Oxford University Press, 2005), xxxv.

13   Machiavelli, *The Prince*, 58.

THE PROBLEM

KEY POINTS

- During the Renaissance,* books were published that discussed how rulers ought to rule, and what an ideal state would look like. These were called "mirrors for princes."*

- The Italian courtier Baldassare Castiglione* and the Italian philosopher Francesco Patrizi* wrote "mirrors for princes" that focused on teaching ethics as a way to improve rulers' behavior.

- Machiavelli rejected this focus on ethics, because it neglected the realities of politics and did not reveal the truths behind political actions.

Core Question

The question asked by Niccolò Machiavelli and his contemporaries was: how ought rulers to rule, and what does that mean for the political community? In his book *Machiavelli's Prince and its Forerunners*, the American historian Allan Gilbert* explained that the style in which *The Prince* was written would have been a familiar format "to the educated men of the sixteenth century."[1] "Instructional manuals" for rulers—or "mirrors for princes," as they were called—were commonplace.[2] These volumes were primarily intended to remind rulers to rule according to ideas of morality,* religion, and justice. It is important to note that "mirrors for princes" all share the widely-held assumption that the *character* of a ruler was extremely important in determining "the well-being of the kingdom."[3] Social and economic factors were largely ignored.

The core question which "mirrors for princes" attempted to

> ❝ The courtier will in every case be able deftly to show the prince how much honour and profit accrue to him and his from justice, liberality, magnanimity, gentleness, and the other virtues that become a good prince; and on the other hand how much infamy and loss proceed from the vices opposed to them. ❞
>
> Baldassare Castiglione, *The Book of the Courtier*

answer was not "what does the ideal political community look like?" but rather, "who is the ideal ruler, from whom the ideal political community will flow?" This idea of power was based on the idea that those who were ruled would eventually come to resemble those above them in the hierarchy. People living under moral rulers would be more moral, and people living under contemptible rulers would be more contemptible. These thinkers had an idea of the "ideal" ruler and "ideal" community, based on Christian ethics of goodness, honesty, and fear of God.

The Participants

Other writers of "mirrors for princes" tended to focus on how kings could be "morally good." The Italian philosopher Francesco Patrizi wrote *The Education of the King* in the 1470s. This provided a model of the "ruler as essentially one who exemplifies and promotes virtue and justice." Patrizi draws an important distinction between the "bad" ruler as an immoral tyrant and the "good" ruler as a virtuous king.[4]

In 1528 the Italian courtier Baldassare Castiglione published *The Book of the Courtier*. The ideas he put forward were the opposite of Machiavelli's. "The perfect courtier," Castiglione argues, "should aim to make his prince a better person, and thereby (we must presume) a better ruler."[5] What qualities does Castiglione list? "Honour and advantages," he writes, "will accrue to him and his family from justice, liberality, magnanimity, and gentleness," and otherwise "[deterred] from evil."[6]

Both Patrizi and Castiglione explored a concept called *virtù*.* They used this term in the sense that we would use the word "virtue" today. A ruler who displays *virtù* is a kind, honest, moral figure who rules selflessly and for the benefit of everyone else. Machiavelli was skeptical. Could it be the case that those who rule are just very good at making themselves appear "virtuous" while actually being devious?

The Contemporary Debate

Machiavelli also used the term *virtù*, but his understanding of its meaning was radically different from Patrizi and Castiglione's. The British political theorist Bernard Crick* argued that Machiavelli used *virtù* to mean the manly virtues of "courage, audacity, skills and civic spirit" rather than simply "goodness."[7] In this way he links back to classical* concepts outlined by the Roman historian Livy.* In doing this Machiavelli was rejecting the moralizing of thinkers like Castiglione and Patrizi, although he did not mention these writers directly. Machiavelli acknowledges that the qualities listed by other writers of "mirrors for princes" are praiseworthy. But he goes on to point out that it "is not necessary for a prince to possess all of the above-mentioned qualities, but it is very necessary for him to appear to possess them."[8] The British historian Quentin Skinner* called this very important insight "the Machiavellian Revolution." With this insight—that appearance is more important than fact—*virtù* lost its moral qualities. It became purely about the prince's power to maintain and preserve his state.

"[Machiavelli] broke … with the dualistic and one-sidedly spiritualizing ethic of Christianity," wrote the German historian Friedrich Meinecke.* Meinecke meant that Machiavelli believed that Christian ethics prioritized a certain unreality—a world that "ought" to exist over the world that "really" exists.[9] In contrast, Machiavelli prioritized "the national interest" over Christian principles. He argued that politics is the art of preserving the state against its enemies, not the art of seeking some kind of spiritual goal. Other writers had very little concept of a "national interest" that was in any way distinct from Christian dogma. This is why Patrizi and Castiglione saw politics and ethics as identical, whereas Machiavelli saw them as distinct.

NOTES

1   Allan Gilbert, *Machiavelli's Prince and its Forerunners* (Durham: Duke University Press, 1938), 15.

2   Gilbert, *Machiavelli's Prince*, 15.

3   Roberto Lambertini, "Mirrors for Princes," in *Encyclopedia of Medieval Philosophy: Philosophy Between 500 and 1500*, ed. Henrik Lagerlund (Amsterdam: Springer Netherlands, 2011), 791.

4   Ronald W. Truman, *Spanish Treatises on Government, Society and Religion in the Time of Philip II* (Leiden: Koninkijke Brill NV, 1999), 23.

5   Frank Lovett, "The Path of the Courtier: Castiglione, Machiavelli, and the Loss of Republican Liberty," *Review of Politics* 74: 596.

6   Baldassare Castiglione, quoted in Frank Lovett, "The Path of the Courtier," 596.

7   Bernard Crick, introduction to *The Discourses* by Niccolò Machiavelli (New York: Penguin Books, 1970), 53.

8   Niccolò Machiavelli, *The Prince* (Oxford: Oxford University Press, 2005), 61.

9   Freidrich Meinecke, *Machiavellism: The Doctrine of Raison d'État and its Place in Modern History* (New Brunswick: Transaction Publishers, 1998), 31.

MODULE 4
THE AUTHOR'S CONTRIBUTION

KEY POINTS

- Some thinkers, including the philosopher Jean-Jacques Rousseau,* believed *The Prince* was a satire* designed to highlight the corrupt nature of people in power. Others disagreed.

- Machiavelli's approach redefined political thought, drawing conclusions from observed data, rather than abstract ideas of "the good."

- Machiavelli is not interested in religious or ethical ideals when discussing political power.

Author's Aims

In the opening dedication of *The Prince*, Niccolò Machiavelli suggests his book will help political leaders be more effective by summarizing and interpreting "the deeds of great men".[1] But whether this was really his aim has been hotly disputed.

In his 1971 article "The Question of Machiavelli," the Russo-British philosopher Isaiah Berlin* notes that there are as many interpretations of Machiavelli's aims as there are scholars of Machiavelli. He notes more than 20 such interpretations. Thinkers throughout history, including the famous Genevan philosopher Jean-Jacques Rousseau, believed Machiavelli wrote *The Prince* as a work of protest, with its true meaning hidden in layers of satire. In his 1762 work *The Social Contract*, Rousseau wrote that Machiavelli's "hidden aim" is revealed to all but "superficial or corrupt readers,"[2] and that Machiavelli aimed to reveal the arbitrary and unjust power wielded by the

> 66 The primary purpose of *The Prince* then is not to give particular counsel to a contemporary Italian prince, but to set forth a wholly new teaching regarding wholly new princes in wholly new states, or a shocking teaching about the most shocking phenomena. 99
>
> Leo Strauss, "Machiavelli's Intention in *The Prince*"

aristocracy* and the Church in Renaissance* Europe. Rousseau concludes that the Vatican prohibited *The Prince* in 1559 because "it is that Court it most clearly portrays" in a critical light.[3] On the other hand, the German American political theorist Leo Strauss* argues that the view that *The Prince* is a satire is mistaken. Strauss believes that Machiavelli's end goal was actually to create a resource for a powerful, ruthless leader to forge a new state out of Italy's bickering cities. "The primary purpose of *The Prince*," argues Strauss, "is ... not to give particular counsel to a contemporary Italian prince, but to set forth a wholly new teaching regarding wholly new princes in wholly new states."[4] In other words, Strauss thinks Machiavelli was concerned with setting out a new kind of political theory based on the naked truth of power, and stripped of its false philosophy.

Approach

Whether it was to teach princes how to rule effectively, or to point out the hypocrisy of the powerful, Machiavelli's intention was to bring cold reality to the study of politics. His approach was grounded in the study of history, rather than thinking about ethics. This was a radically different approach for the time of the Renaissance.

Machiavelli argues that when conquering a new state, a prince "should weigh all the injurious [cruel] things he must do and commit them all at once," rather than slowly and over time. In support of this argument Machiavelli examines the experience of an ancient Greek tyrant called Agathocles.* Having taken over the government of the city of Syracuse in Sicily, Agathocles "had his troops kill all the senators and the richest citizens,"[5] to secure his position. This policy worked and allowed Agathocles to maintain his rule. Using him as an example, Machiavelli creates a general principle that people who are to rule must do some things that appear wrong and that they should do what they do quickly and efficiently, rather than give any possible opponents a chance to organize themselves. This advice is important, because it is not an instruction "from above": from either religion or philosophy. Instead it is derived "from below." Like a scientific inquiry, it is derived from the study of real events.

Contribution In Context

The Prince is without question an original piece of work. It is true that its format—the "mirror for princes"* style of writing—was borrowed from Machiavelli's contemporaries. And in his famous work *Utopia* (1516), the English statesman Thomas More* did make a similar observation to Machiavelli. More wrote: "most kings are more interested in the science of war ... than in useful peacetime techniques. They're far more anxious, by hook or by crook, to acquire new kingdoms than to govern their existing ones properly."[6] Both More and Machiavelli see this as ineffective rule, but for different reasons. More advises princes to operate from the basis of being "good;" Machiavelli says their primary concern must be holding and maintaining power.

In general, however, *The Prince* was unlike anything written by Machiavelli's contemporaries. As political thinker Isaiah Berlin said, Machiavelli is primarily concerned with "completely [ignoring] the concepts and categories ... in terms of which the best-known thinkers and scholars of his day were accustomed to expressing themselves."[7]

Machiavelli's contemporaries were preoccupied with the question of how princes could be moral, honest and religious. In contrast, Machiavelli argued that princes should concern themselves *only* with the real issues of gaining and maintaining power. He makes no reference to any ideals—religious or otherwise—in his account of political power as a natural gain from being a good person. "There is nothing [in *The Prince*]," Berlin wrote, "of the idea of teleology."*[8] "Teleology" comes from Greek, and can be understood as "the logic (logos) of the end (telos)." Teleology assumes everything is defined by some "perfect" end state. But Machiavelli believed it was only important for princes to "appear" moral, honest, and religious, and that the only political judgment that would be passed on someone would be based on either their success or failure to maintain power. The prince's personality, therefore, was only important inasmuch as it enabled him to be ruthless.

NOTES

1   Niccolò Machiavelli, *The Prince* (London: Penguin Books, 2003), 3.

2   Jean-Jacques Rousseau, *The Social Contract* (New York: Cosimo, 2008), 74.

3   Rousseau, *Social Contract*, 74.

4   Leo Strauss, "Machiavelli's Intention in *The Prince*," *The American Political Science Review* 51, no. 1 (1957): 34.

5   Niccolò Machiavelli, *The Prince* (Oxford: Oxford University Press, 2005), 31.

6   Thomas More, *Utopia* (London: Penguin Books, 1965), 42.

7   Isaiah Berlin, "The Originality of Machiavelli," in *Against the Current: Essays in the History of Ideas* (Princeton: Princeton University Press, 2013), 36–37.

8   Berlin, "Originality of Machiavelli," 37.

SECTION 2
IDEAS

MODULE 5
MAIN IDEAS

KEY POINTS

- The key themes of *The Prince* are power, *"virtù,"** and the relationship of morality* to politics.

- Machiavelli says princes should concern themselves exclusively with gaining and maintaining power. Moral "goodness" is only important as a show.

- Machiavelli wrote in Italian (rather than Latin) and presented his thoughts in a very direct way. He wanted his readers to think about politics in a very practical way.

Key Themes

The most important theme in Niccolò Machiavelli's *The Prince* is power: the nature of power, how power can be gained, and the forces that shape the lives of the powerful.

Machiavelli argues that three forces can shape the life of a powerful man: *virtù, necessità** and *fortuna.** *Virtù* is the ability to act effectively. *Neccesità* is necessity—the ability to adapt to changing circumstances. *Fortuna* is fate or luck.

These three forces can be understood by using an analogy. Imagine a prince with a neighbor whose power is increasing. If the prince possesses *virtù* he will carry out a pre-emptive strike, killing the neighboring prince before he can become a threat. *Necessità* calls for a reactive strike, killing the neighboring prince after he has become a threat. The decision representing *fortuna* is no decision at all. It is registering a moral objection to killing, and then patiently waiting for the neighboring prince to die from a heart attack before he attacks. Machiavelli would understand this "moral" prince, a man whose

> **❝ A Prince must not have any other object nor any other thought, nor must he adopt anything as his art but war. ❞**
>
> Machiavelli, *The Prince*

actions are most likely constrained by his religion and his sense of honor, as a man who relies almost entirely on *fortuna* for his position as a ruler. In Machiavelli's eyes this prince cannot be relied on to govern a principality.

Machiavelli believed that, for better or for worse, politics and morality were not the same thing. In fact, they were often totally incompatible. The measure of a ruler's worth is not goodness. It's how well he can adapt to new circumstances and how well he can anticipate those circumstances. Effective rulers use morality as a convenient fiction to dupe lesser men.

These ideas were shocking to early modern* audiences, who understood their entire social and political lives to be divinely ordered: that is, mapped out by God. As a result, Machiavelli was portrayed as an evil figure. In boasting of his own wickedness, William Shakespeare's* Richard III says he can "set the murderous Machiavel to school."[1]

Exploring The Ideas

Machiavelli said princes should not concern themselves with having a moral, just, or kind rule. Nor should they worry about the well-being of their subjects any more than ensuring that their contentedness will stop them from rising against him. "A Prince," Machiavelli argues, "must not have any other object nor any other thought, nor must he adopt anything as his art but war."[2] In other words, the prince should focus on maintaining his power, or gaining power from others who are not strong enough to prevent him from doing so. Machiavelli's advice emphasizes ruthlessness and entirely fails to mention justice.

He completely separates morality from politics.

This separation of morals and politics is at its clearest when Machiavelli lists the virtues of the ruthless Italian nobleman Cesare Borgia.* Borgia protected himself from his enemies, conquered "by force or deceit," made himself "loved and feared by the people," wiped out "those who [meant him] harm," and was utterly pragmatic.[3] Machiavelli's list lacks any mention of ethics or religious sensibility. But Cesare Borgia was the best ruler Machiavelli could name, and he ruled for the benefit and glory of none other than Cesare Borgia.

This point is illustrated by Machiavelli's discussion of generosity. It is necessary to *seem* generous, Machiavelli argues, but it is not practical to be generous with one's own resources. "Of what is not yours, or your subjects'," Machiavelli says, "you can be a more generous donor."[4] In other words, princes should benefit from appearing generous (and so being thought to be virtuous) by plundering from others and being generous with *their* resources. In this way, "generosity" in a moral sense (desiring to do good) and "generosity" in a political sense (being selectively generous from a desire to *seem* good) become completely distinct.

Language And Expression

Machiavelli's style is clear and stark. In the book's opening dedication he says that he has not "embellished or crammed this book with rounded periods or big impressive words."[5] The philosopher Isaiah Berlin* believes this is part of the reason why *The Prince* has been an important book for so long. "*The Prince* is a short book ... singularly lucid, succinct and pungent—a model of clear Renaissance* prose."[6] It was written quickly, in an emotional outburst and the text reflects Machiavelli's changing emotional state. He saw his own position in the Florentine court under threat while Italy, once the center of the Western world, was suffering at the hands of fractious city-states ruled by inept princes.

Although he occasionally combines specialized Latin terms with colloquial Florentine language, most of *The Prince* is written in straightforward, direct language, which makes it feel as though Machiavelli is talking directly to the reader. Indeed, he hoped the text would impress, shock, and even advise his readers. He wanted to direct their attention to his practical political experience, which he presented as a necessary antidote to fanciful dreams of imaginary states. He is, however, very critical of failed leaders. In discussing these men, Machiavelli's writing takes on a scathing, sarcastic, and contemptuous tone. Yet his political enthusiasm always shines through, making the text extremely persuasive. Furthermore, his concise and clever style makes *The Prince* very quotable and the writing lingers long after reading.

NOTES

1   William Shakespeare, *Henry VI Part Three*, 3.2.109, in *The Complete Works by William Shakespeare* (Oxford: Oxford University Press, 1994), 109.

2   Niccolò Machiavelli, *The Prince* (Oxford: Oxford University Press, 2005), 50.

3   Machiavelli, *The Prince*, 29–30.

4   Machiavelli, *The Prince*, 56.

5   Niccolò Machiavelli, *The Prince* (London: Penguin Books, 2003), 3.

6   Isaiah Berlin, "A Special Supplement: The Question of Machiavelli," *New York Review of Books*, November 4, 1971, accessed December 11, 2014, http://www.nybooks.com/articles/archives/1971/nov/04/a-special-supplement-the-question-of-machiavelli/.

MODULE 6
SECONDARY IDEAS

KEY POINTS

- Machiavelli's work has been interpreted as viewing political realism as acceptable if it preserves the state.
- Understanding Machiavelli in this new light suggests he was as much a patriot as he was a political thinker.
- Machiavelli has recently been reinterpreted as one of the first "political scientists," by focusing on the importance of realities rather than ethics.

Other Ideas

Niccolò Machiavelli's core idea in *The Prince* is a negative one. He sets out to disprove the idea that political power is founded on a leader's morality* or moral worth. His aim is political realism. But many scholars believe that Machiavelli intended his book to be much more than this. They believe he had a "hidden" intention—a desire to promote the "raison d'état"* or "the national interest." These scholars argue that in *The Prince*, Machiavelli was suggesting that "any behavior, however apparently immoral, was justified if its goal was to preserve the state."[1]

It is important to remember that "the state" as it is understood now did not exist while Machiavelli was writing. In his time, states were not "solid" units in the way that modern states are understood to be. They were more fluid and more reliant on the personalities of their leaders. While leaders controlled territory, they also owed allegiance to outside powers themselves, the Roman Catholic Church,* for example. Yet in formulating the idea of some kind of "national interest," the British historian Quentin Skinner* argued that Machiavelli could be seen as

> **❝** Virtue will seize arms
> Against frenzy, and the battle will be brief:
> For ancient valour
> Is not yet dead in Italian hearts. **❞**
> Petrarch, quoted in Machiavelli, *The Prince*

an early theorist of the idea of state sovereignty.* Sovereign states are those which govern themselves and are independent from foreign interference.

Machiavelli is also sometimes seen as an early theorist of liberal* politics. Liberalism today is defined as a political philosophy that favors individual liberty, free trade and moderate political and social reform. This is a long way from Machiavelli's ideas. But his rejection of "tradition for tradition's sake" (or "morality for morality's sake") means *The Prince* can also be read as an early liberal book, insofar as it provides an account of political life based on observation of reality, rather than reflection on tradition. It is a way of looking at politics that allows for more individual choice. Princes should do what is best based on what they *need* to do in the circumstances, rather than obeying a set of abstract rules.

Exploring The Ideas

Toward the end of the book Machiavelli wonders, "whether at present in Italy … there is the material that might give a prudent and virtuous prince" the opportunity to "put an end to the plundering of Lombardy" (referring to France's invasion of Lombardy in 1494) and otherwise free Italy from foreign influence.[2] Moreover, he ends his volume with a challenge to the house of Medici* to "take up this task with the spirit and the hope with which just enterprises are begun, so that under your banner this country may be ennobled."[3]

Why is this significant? The German American historian Felix

Gilbert,* in his famous essay "The Concept of Nationalism in Machiavelli's Prince," wrote "there is a striking difference between the emotional idealism which pervades the national appeal of the last chapter of *The Prince* and the cold and realistic analysis of political forces which forms the distinguishing feature of the rest of the work."[4] Does this mean, as some scholars have argued, that Machiavelli's work is a "how to" guide to the future liberator of Italy? These scholars suggest that Machiavelli is arguing that a strong ruler should create a modern nation-state out of Italy's patchwork of feuding cities.

According to the Italian academic Maurizio Viroli,* "the most compelling evidence for the rhetorical* nature of *The Prince*"[5] (in effect its desire to persuade the reader) is its final emotional chapter. "Without it," Viroli goes on, "Machiavelli's essay would have lacked the device which is most necessary in order to arouse the reader's emotions and move them to do what he was urging them to accomplish."[6]

It is important to note that this interpretation of Machiavelli's last chapter as a call for a modern nation state is not universally accepted. But it is one of many competing interpretations outlined by Felix Gilbert.

Overlooked

The difficulty in studying Machiavelli is less one of neglect and more one of interpretation. Some modern thinkers, most notably the American academic Allan Bloom,* have included Machiavelli among the Enlightenment* philosophers, even though the Enlightenment was generally very critical of him.[7] Bloom believes a close reading of Machiavelli reveals "the inspirer of the great philosophical systems of modernity".[8] By implementing a "daring innovation ... modern philosophy was to be politically effective."[9] Whereas pre-modern philosophy focused on ethics, morals, and a "given" idea of the good life, Bloom argues that "Machiavelli dared men literally to forget about their souls and the possibility of eternal damnation," and to theorize only about those things that could be sensed.[10]

One of the most telling passages about this is Machiavelli's famous line, "there is such a distance between how one lives and how one ought to live, that anyone who abandons what is done for what ought to be done achieves his downfall rather than his preservation."[11] What Machiavelli means by this is that political survival requires leaders to ignore what "ought" to be done. For Bloom, this isn't a rejection of "goodness." It's about acknowledging politics as it really is and recognizing that facts are more important than morals. This evidence-driven methodology (rather than a morally reflective methodology) is why thinkers like Bloom and the American academic Harvey Mansfield* suggest that Machiavelli was among the first "scientists" of politics.[12]

In this interpretation of the work, rather than denying the importance of ethics, Machiavelli wants to build up the importance of "real things." He is, therefore, the first real political "scientist" of modernity. While this idea is certainly radical and interesting, there has been no general acceptance of it.

NOTES

1   Victoria Kahn, "Machiavelli's Reputation to the Eighteenth Century," in *The Cambridge Companion to Machiavelli*, ed. John M. Najemy (Cambridge: Cambridge University Press, 2010), 245.

2   Niccolò Machiavelli, *The Prince* (Oxford: Oxford University Press, 2005), 87–88.

3   Machiavelli, *The Prince*, 90.

4   Felix Gilbert, "The Concept of Nationalism in Machiavelli's Prince," *Studies in the Renaissance* 1 (1954): 38.

5   Maruizio Viroli, introduction to *The Prince* by Niccolò Machiavelli (Oxford: Oxford University Press, 2005), xxv.

6   Viroli, introduction, xxv.

7   Allan Bloom, *Closing of the American Mind* (New York: Simon and Schuster, 1987), 263.

8   Bloom, *Closing*, 263.

9   Bloom, *Closing*, 263.

10   Bloom, *Closing*, 174.

11   Machiavelli, *The Prince*, 52.

12   Harvey C. Mansfield, "Machiavelli's Political Science," *The American Political Science Review* 75, no. 2 (1981): 293.

MODULE 7
ACHIEVEMENT

KEY POINTS

- *The Prince* is much more than a simple guide to how to be ruthless. It encourages readers to look at politics based on facts above all.

- The book was banned by the Roman Catholic Church* in 1559, but it is likely that this only encouraged the general public to want to read it.

- Some thinkers have suggested that leaders who criticized *The Prince* as unethical were only doing it to appear ethical themselves.

Assessing The Argument

Niccolò Machiavelli's *The Prince* is still relevant to contemporary politics. This is because of its clear approach, its universal ideas and the insights Machiavelli offers into political leadership. It is relevant because it deals with an essential question: what, in reality, makes for successful rule?

The Prince is distinctive because it is one of the few works on leadership (and certainly one of the earliest) that approaches the subject without ideological and moral baggage. It addresses the key issue of how to maintain power with a directness that few other works match.

As a result, Machiavelli's name has become identified with cunning. In the 1960s the term "Machiavellianism"* started to be used to describe particularly manipulative personalities, people "lacking in interpersonal affect, low [concern] with conventional morality* … low ideological commitment."[1] The social psychologists who coined

> 66 *New York Times:* **If you could require the President to read one book, what would it be? Jared Diamond:** *The Prince..*99
>
> Jared Diamond, interview with the *New York Times*, 2013 ("Jared Diamond: By the Book")

this term, Richard Christie* and Florence Geis,* explained that they used it because, "Since the publication of *The Prince* in 1532, the name of its author has come to designate the use of deceit in politics."[2] However, seeing *The Prince* as nothing more than a "how to" guide for individuals who are willing to act amorally ignores many of Machiavelli's achievements. His work was key in establishing political science as a distinctive discipline, while also showing a "just the facts" approach to politics.

Achievement In Context

The Prince was successful despite being denounced by the Church. The Canadian academic Michael Ignatieff* notes that the book "was placed on the Papal Index* of banned books in 1559, and its author was denounced on the … stages of London as the 'Evil Machiavel.'[3]"[4] The British academic John Roe* has studied the relationship between Machiavellian ideas and popular drama. He believes the Papal ban on *The Prince* "only guaranteed its popularity since it appeared … in a Latin translation"[5] shortly after. It was then reprinted three times before 1600.

In relating one anecdote as to how the first copies of *The Prince* appeared in England, Roe illustrates exactly how exciting the book was. One printer "brought out an Italian edition of [*The Prince*] in London in 1584, the title page claiming Palermo as the place of publication … Such audacity attests to the demand for the book."[6] The English would have considered it scandalous to print the book in

England, so it was a necessary fiction to pretend that it had been printed in Palermo. Roe argues that while critics despised *The Prince*, the general public was excited about it. This may go a long way to explain why such a widely criticized book survived. People may have been drawn to *The Prince* precisely because it was widely condemned.

Limitations

All Machiavelli's work was widely read when it was first published, but *The Prince* was especially popular. Many of its readers did not react to Machiavelli's ideas, however. Instead, they reacted to the "cartoon version" of Machiavelli, the figure of evil.

Yet when rulers dismissed *The Prince*, was it because they misinterpreted Machiavelli, or because they were following his advice? Frederick II,* who ruled the northern European kingdom of Prussia during the eighteenth century, noted that "Machiavelli ... upon seeing the balance [of power] settled in Europe by the alliance of many princes and states against the over-powerful and ambitious, a balance solely designed for securing the peace and tranquility of mankind,"[7] would have believed that his own theory of politics was outdated. Frederick's opinion was that good politics would reduce conflict and so avoid the need to be "Machiavellian" altogether. However, the network of alliances that had created this balance of power was itself the result of cold, calculating Machiavellian logic. In addition, it was in Frederick's best interests to attack Machiavelli's work. Machiavelli had said that rulers needed to *appear* to be ethical. By condemning Machiavelli, Frederick appeared actually to *be* ethical. So despite his apparent criticism of *The Prince*, Frederick II was effectively following its advice.

This was not the first or the last time that a negative judgment would be passed on Machiavelli. However, as the centuries passed, it did start to become less common to dismiss Machiavelli as nothing more than a criminal or a teacher of evil.

NOTES

1   Richard Christie and Florence Geis, *Studies in Machiavellianism* (New York: Academic Press, 1970). 4.

2   Christie and Geis, *Studies*, 1.

3   See William Shakespeare, *Henry VI Part Three*, 3.2.109, in *The Complete Works* by William Shakespeare (Oxford: Oxford University Press, 1994), 109.

4   Michael Ignatieff, "Machiavelli Was Right," *The Atlantic*, December 2013, accessed December 28, 2014, http://www.theatlantic.com/magazine/archive/2013/12/machiavelli-was-right/354672/?single_page=true.

5   John Allan Roe, *Shakespeare and Machiavelli* (Cambridge: D. S. Brewer, 2002) 3–4.

6   Roe, *Shakespeare and Machiavelli*, 4.

7   Jay Luvaas, *Frederick the Great on the Art of War* (New York: The Free Press, 1999), 36.

MODULE 8
PLACE IN THE AUTHOR'S WORK

KEY POINTS

- In his most important works Machiavelli examined different ways in which political bodies could be organized.

- Some thinkers believe that buried in *The Prince* are the seeds of the political movement that became known as liberalism.*

- The famous philosopher Francis Bacon* saw *The Prince* as important because it explains how evil men can rise to power. He hopes this knowledge will lead to good men being less easily deceived.

Positioning

Niccolò Machiavelli wrote *The Prince* in 1513, when he was 44. This was relatively late in his life and the book was intended to sum up his experiences as a political figure in his native Florence. Machiavelli's most famous works all dealt with the subject of politics—including *The Art of War* (1521) and *The Discourses on Livy** (1531). Politics was at the heart of some of his less well-known works too, such as *Discourse on Pisa* (1499). He did try his hand at other things, writing a number of plays including (most famously) *The Mandrake* (1524), a comedy in which a young man attempts to seduce the attractive wife of an old man.

Machiavelli's two most important works, though, are *The Prince* and *The Discourses on Livy*. *The Discourses* is a book about the rise of a free republic. "Experience," says Machiavelli in *The Discourses*, "shows that cities have never increased in dominion or riches except while they have been at liberty."[1] Yet in *The Prince* Machiavelli is offering advice to rulers who want to gain and hold onto power—and maintain

> ❝ When it is a question of the safety of one's fatherland, there must be no consideration of just or unjust, of merciful or cruel, of praiseworthy or disgraceful; instead, setting aside every scruple, one must follow to the utmost any plan that will save her life and keep her liberty. ❞
>
> Machiavelli, *Discourses on Livy*

their power over cities.

This seems at odds with Machiavelli's argument in *The Discourses*. However, when Machiavelli outlines how republics gain and hold onto power, the common themes between the two books emerge. Machiavelli says, "When it is absolutely a question of the safety of one's country ... there must be no consideration of the just or unjust, of merciful or cruel, of praiseworthy or disgraceful." Instead, the sole focus should be only on what is necessary to preserve the city.[2] In other words, republics are no more moral than other political systems. What is different about republics is rather the relationship between the state and its citizens.

Integration

The Russo-British philosopher Isaiah Berlin* described how modern political philosophy has a generally difficult relationship with Machiavelli. "There is no consensus about the significance of either [*The Prince* or *The Discourses*]; they have not been absorbed into the texture of traditional political theory; they continue to arouse passionate feelings."[3] This is especially true, Berlin notes, among those involved in politics. Whether *The Prince* was a satire,* a patriotic rallying cry, or a piece of pure philosophy, Berlin concludes that its "intellectual consequences ... were ... the basis of the very liberalism that Machiavelli would surely have condemned as feeble."[4]

What does Berlin mean by this? Machiavelli offers lessons to the powerful on how to retain power. He reveals how useful belief systems are in upholding power. A system of beliefs based on a strict loyalty to Christianity, for example, defined the lives of nearly everyone in Renaissance* Italy. Machiavelli presents the idea that there is no universal truth; there are only the truths enforced by the powerful, to support their own interests. Berlin argues that this leads to liberalism because, "Toleration is historically the product of the realization of the irreconcilability of equally dogmatic faiths, and the practical improbability of complete victory of one over the other."[5]

This means that as soon as we realize that one belief system is as likely to be true as another, then we start on the road to tolerating them all equally. Toleration is at the root of a liberal society. This, according to Berlin, is why it's possible to argue that *The Prince* may be viewed as the first almost-liberal work. It also shows why Machiavelli was not contradicting himself when he wrote about different forms of government in *The Prince* and *The Discourses*.

Significance

The Prince is one of the most famous political works in the world. It was among the first post-Classical* books to make bold statements about the realities of power and politics. It was also groundbreaking in the way it discarded the moralizing that characterized most other work of the time.

Yet the academic significance of *The Prince* remains hotly debated. Scholars still disagree about whether *The Prince* is a work of satire, a work of liberalism, or simply a how-to guide for evil. "There is something surprising," argues Berlin, "about the sheer number of interpretations of Machiavelli's political opinions. There exist, even now, over a score of leading theories of how to interpret *The Prince* and *The Discourses*"—and this body of work is growing constantly.[6]

In many ways, *The Prince* is still important precisely because there is so much room for debate over what Machiavelli was really saying. Of the early modern* interpretations of Machiavelli, however, it is the sixteenth-century English philosopher Francis Bacon who perhaps does him the most justice:"we are much beholden to Machiavelli and others, that write what men do and not what they ought to do," because without knowledge of "the forms and natures of evil ... virtue lieth open and unfenced."[7] Bacon means that we need a clear account of how evil men can seize power—especially if they do so while appearing virtuous. For without this, good men will be easily deceived.

NOTES

1 Niccolò Machiavelli, *The Discourses on Livy*, quoted in *Machiavelli* by Quentin Skinner (Oxford: Oxford University Press, 1981), 51.

2 Niccolò Machiavelli, *The Discourses on Livy*, quoted in *Reading Political Philosophy: Machiavelli to Mill* by Nigel Warburton et al. (Abingdon: Routledge, 2006), 52.

3 Isaiah Berlin, "A Special Supplement: The Question of Machiavelli," *New York Review of Books*, November 4, 1971, accessed December 11, 2014, http:/www.nybooks.com/articles/archives/1971/nov/04/a-special-supplement-the-question-of-machiavelli/.

4 Berlin, "The Question."

5 Berlin, "The Question."

6 Berlin, "The Question."

7 Francis Bacon, *The Advancement of Learning*, ed. Arthur Johnston (Oxford: Oxford University Press, 1974), 157.

SECTION 3
IMPACT

MODULE 9
THE FIRST RESPONSES

KEY POINTS

- *The Prince* spawned an entire genre of political "anti-Machiavel" thought, where the ideas in the book were blamed for the scheming that caused religious wars.
- In the nineteenth century scholars, especially the German philosopher G. W. F. Hegel,* began to bring Machiavelli into mainstream thought as both a liberal* and an early republican.
- German nationalists in the late nineteenth century looked at Machiavelli's views to support their desire for a German state. This gave birth to the idea of "realpolitik."*

Criticism

The German historian Friedrich Meinecke* noted that Niccolò Machiavelli's *The Prince* sparked serious controversy. The first near-contemporary response to Machiavelli after the book was published in 1513 came from a French jurist and political thinker, Innocent Gentillet.* Gentillet wrote a book called *Anti Machiavel* (Machiavelli's name was often shortened to Machiavel). He saw the kind of thinking Machiavelli explored in *The Prince* as largely responsible for the unrest in France around the time of the Religious Wars* of the sixteenth century. These civil wars between Roman Catholics* and Protestant Huguenots* broke out in 1562, which was 30 years after the first printed version of Machiavelli's text became available. "Machiavelli," Gentillet declared, "recommended that one should sow dissension amongst one's subjects"[1] and therefore undermine the political community. For Gentillet, the religious strife in France had arisen, not

> 66 Machiavelli's theory was a sword which was plunged into the flank of the body politic of Western humanity, causing it to shriek and rear up ... for not only had genuine moral feeling been seriously wounded, but death had also been threatened to the Christian views of all churches and sects. 99
>
> Friedrich Meinecke, *Machiavellism: The Doctrine of Raison d'État and its Place in Modern History*

out of genuine religious tension, but from a Machiavellian scheme at the highest levels of power. Gentillet's argument, however, was poor. "His attack," writes Meinecke, "was clumsy, [wordy], and full of misconceptions."[2]

Yet Gentillet was far from Machiavelli's only critic. In fact, his views were representative of the way *The Prince* was seen in early modern* Europe. Machiavelli's ideas weren't given much serious consideration and were simply attacked as evil. As Meinecke pointed out, this happened because powerful men who benefitted from the status quo "... suddenly realised that [their] whole world and way of life were threatened"[3] by Machiavelli's exposure of how politics really worked. In other words, Machiavelli argued that rulers' claims to rule were based on nothing more than power. There was no "right" or "goodness" inherent in any one political system.

Responses

Machiavelli's book has generally been better received as politics has become increasingly distinct from religion and ethics. However, this change in perception did not really come about until the nineteenth century. G. W. F. Hegel was a key figure in bringing about this change. He applauded what he saw as Machiavelli's "basic aim of raising Italy to statehood."[4] What does he mean by this? Hegel's interpretation of

Machiavelli was as a thinker who saw his country damaged by conflict, wracked by wars between cities, and ruled by petty princes who lacked the *virtù** to forge a nation. Hegel believed that Machiavelli was actually critical of Italy's cruel rulers in *The Prince*. As a result, he dismissed those critics who were "short-sighted enough to regard [the book] as no more than the foundation for tyranny or a golden mirror for an ambitious oppressor."[5]

Hegel saw that Cesare Borgia,* "the man whom Machiavelli had hoped to see as the saviour of Italy ... had constructed a state" out of a patchwork of minor principalities.[6] Hegel praises Machiavelli for accepting that Borgia needed to commit injustices in order to build a strong state out of this patchwork. He wrote: "what would indeed be abhorrent if done by one private individual to another, or by one state to another" is forgivable when done in service of the state's highest—and indeed only—duty, which is "to preserve itself."[7] Hegel's view of Machiavelli is consistent with an early theory of sovereignty,* that there is no higher authority than the state. Therefore states owe no duty to any entity but themselves. Hegel was arguing that Machiavelli was no villain. Instead, the Italian thinker was the first theorist of the sovereign state.*

Conflict And Consensus

Hegel was not the only German thinker who viewed Machiavelli's work in a positive light. In the early nineteenth century, Germany was not a united country. It was part of the Holy Roman Empire, an association of small principalities that extended over much of Central Europe, including what is now Germany and northern Italy. German nationalists believed it was wrong that the German "nation" (people who shared a common language, ancestry and sense of national identity) was split up into bickering states. They wanted to forge a nation. The Canadian academic Robert Howse* writes, "The rehabilitation of Machiavelli and his exoneration from being a teacher of evil by the German nationalists were based on a conception of a state [over all]."[8]

This desire for a German state was based on a belief that while a fragmented Germany may have been good for the individual rulers, it was generally bad for the German people. In 1871, the Prussian statesman Otto von Bismarck* achieved the nationalists' goal and created the German Empire. Writing about Bismarck, the American historian Otto Pflanze* said, "Like Machiavelli, Bismarck concluded that the essence of politics is power," and, moreover, that ideals had no power of their own.[9] It was in Germany that the word describing a Machiavellian approach to politics arose: realpolitik. This means "the politics of real things."

Ruthlessness in the service of state-building was familiar to Bismarck. "Germany is not looking to Prussia's liberalism," he said in a famous speech, "but to its power" to lead Germany with "blood and iron."[10] This echoes the way Machiavelli dismissed the idea of morality* as the key to political success. Those who wanted to forge a German state in the nineteenth century knew—as Machiavelli did in fifteenth-century Florence—that "in circumstances of fundamental weakness, there is a necessity of using the most brutal means to create a strong, healthy state."[11] In other words, as politics became more depersonalized, and the importance of the sovereign state grew, Machiavelli was seen in an increasingly favorable light.

NOTES

1   Freidrich Meinecke, *Machiavellism: The Doctrine of Raison d'État and its Place in Modern History* (New Brunswick: Transaction Publishers, 1998), 52.

2   Meinecke, *Machiavellism*, 52.

3   Meinecke, *Machiavellism*, 54.

4   G. W. F. Hegel, *The German Constitution*, accessed December 14, 2014, https://www.marxists.org/reference/archive/hegel/works/gc/ch02.htm.

5   Hegel, *German Constitution*.

6   Hegel, *German Constitution*.

7   Hegel, *German Constitution*.

8   Robert Howse, *Leo Strauss: Man of Peace* (Cambridge: Cambridge University Press, 2014), 93.

9   Otto Pflanze, "Bismarck's Realpolitik," *The Review of Politics* 20, no. 4 (1958): 493.

10 Otto von Bismarck, "Blood and Iron Speech," accessed December 14, 2014, http://germanhistorydocs.ghi-dc.org/sub_document.cfm?document_id=250.

11 Howse, *Strauss*, 93.

MODULE 10
THE EVOLVING DEBATE

KEY POINTS

- Some thinkers believe Machiavelli was the first person to distinguish between facts and value in the political arena. He believed that someone's personal moral code should not dictate their political decision-making, but rather facts alone.

- Early liberal* thought arose from Machiavelli's "scientific" approach to politics. It continues to help define the school of realism* in international relations.*

- It is politicians rather than academics or philosophers who have been most drawn to *The Prince*'s ideas.

Uses And Problems

The influence of *The Prince* has been profound. Niccolò Machiavelli has been credited as the first major Western thinker to illuminate the "fact–value distinction."*[1] This is the difference between facts (which can be discovered by observing reality) and values (which can be constructed through moral reflection). It is a fact that shooting a gun at someone will badly injure them. It is a value to believe that badly injuring someone is bad, so one should not shoot guns.

Before *The Prince*, medieval* theorists like Saint Augustine* would use their moral judgments to determine what the ideal society would be—an "imagined principality." For Augustine, society was given to men by God so they might become morally uplifted.[2] But Machiavelli argued that men should not be bound by ethical constraints (values) to do "foolish" things (neglect facts).[3] He argued that society was not the expression of higher values like goodness and justice. Observation

> **❝** The condition of man ... is a condition of war of every one against every one; in which case everyone is governed by his own Reason; and there is nothing he can make use of, that may not be a help unto him, in preserving his life against his enemies. **❞**
>
> Thomas Hobbes, *Leviathan*

showed that society was, in fact, the result of lower instincts, such as hunger and violence.

Machiavelli's ideas influenced later thinkers. The seventeenth-century English philosopher Thomas Hobbes* based his theory of the state on the idea of the "social contract."* He argued that men would create states because living in a state is more comfortable than living in a state of nature. By the "state of nature" Hobbes means humans living as animals and competing for resources to satisfy their needs: a "war of all against all."[4] Hobbes's theory was based on facts about humanity. He believed that humans need to restrain their natural capacity for cruelty and betrayal. He called his theory "the social contract," because it involved groups of humans creating society themselves, for their own benefit, by mutual agreement.

Schools Of Thought

In the twentieth century Machiavelli's ideas on the unchanging nature of man, the separation of politics from ethics and the overriding importance of "necessity" went on to inform realism in international relations.*.[5] This can be seen in the work of the British historian E. H. Carr,* who wrote that in international affairs, "every political situation contains mutually incompatible elements of utopia* and reality, of morality* and power."[6] He rejects the idea that a moral framework can curb one's own interests and that paradise can be found through mutual trust and cooperation. His book *The Twenty Years' Crisis* shows the distinction between fact and value is alive and well in the twentieth century.

Realism holds that relations between states are based solely on the balance of power. Therefore peace can only be achieved if one state becomes more powerful than all the others put together. "The utopia of Machiavelli," according to the German American academic Hans Morgenthau,* would be a "stable, peaceful society" of states in international relations, "built on power alone."[7] Morgenthau wrote about international politics and, like Machiavelli, he argued that nations should not confuse morality with survival. "Realism," Morgenthau argues, "considers prudence—the weighing of the consequences of alternative political actions—to be the supreme virtue in politics."[8] A pragmatic statesman does not ask: "what is the right thing to do for my ideology," but rather, "how does this policy affect the power of the nation?"[9]

This is classic Machiavellianism,* but Machiavelli was not the first thinker in this tradition. The ancient Greek historian Thucydides* is often credited as being the first realist political thinker. A passage in his book, *The History of the Peloponnesian War*, reports a discussion between the strong Athenians, and the weak Melians, in which it is stated that: "Questions of justice only arise when there is equal power to compel."[10] Justice (or morality) is only relevant when neither side can dominate the other. Otherwise, as the Athenians say to the Melians, "the dominant exact what they can and the weak concede what they must."[11]

In Current Scholarship

A number of academics have looked closely at Machiavelli. There are those who see *The Prince* as a viable target for criticism, including the German American political philosopher Leo Strauss.* And there are those who aim to re-present Machiavelli as an early liberal, such as the Italian academic Maurizio Viroli.* But Machiavelli's real disciples are politicians. Karl Rove,* a senior official in the administration of US President George W. Bush,* is said to have used the teachings of *The Prince* in his approach to American politics. The American reporter Paul Alexander* said, "Rove told people the book he read regularly, perhaps as often as once a year, was *The Prince* by Niccolò Machiavelli."[12] Quoting a colleague of Rove's, Alexander suggests that Rove modelled his "scorched earth"* approach to political campaigning on *The Prince*. In his biography of Rove, Alexander suggests that Rove was willing to do or say anything to win elections and defeat his opponents. But this Machiavellian streak ended up tarnishing his reputation. Another American reporter, John Nichols* wrote an article about Rove called "The Machiavelli Who Failed." This painted a picture of Rove as a politician whose ruthlessness ultimately thwarted his own aims. According to Nichols, Rove only fulfilled one of Machiavelli's two criteria: he was willing to do evil, but he was not able to *appear* to do good. Nichols cites one US politician as saying, "Mr. Rove's apparent attempts to manipulate elections ... shows corruption of federal law enforcement for partisan political purposes."[13] This illustrates the way that Machiavelli's advice still resonates. But it also shows how difficult it is to truly be his disciple in the twenty-first century when media scrutiny makes it much more difficult to appear good, while in fact acting otherwise.

NOTES

1   Harvey C. Mansfield, "Machiavelli's Political Science," *The American Political Science Review* 75, no. 2 (1981): 293.

2   Saint Augustine of Hippo, *The City of God* (Edinburgh: T. & T. Clark, 1841), 1.

3   Isaiah Berlin, "A Special Supplement: The Question of Machiavelli," *New York Review of Books,* November 4, 1971, accessed December 11, 2014, http://www.nybooks.com/articles/archives/1971/nov/04/a-special-supplement-the-question-of-machiavelli/.

4   Thomas Hobbes, *Leviathan* (Digireads Classics, 2009), 85.

5   Classic realist works include E.H. Carr, *The Twenty Years' Crisis, 1919–*
    1939: An Introduction to Study International Relations, (New York: Palgrave,
    2001) and Hans J. Morgenthau, *Politics among Nations: The Struggle for*
    Power and Peace, 2nd ed (New York: Alfred A. Knopf, 1954) with later works
    by Kenneth Waltz, *Theory of International Politics* (Boston, MA: McGraw-Hill
    1979). For a good overview see Jack Donnelly, *Realism and International*
    Relations (Cambridge: Cambridge University Press, 2000).

6   E. H. Carr, *The Twenty Years' Crisis: An Introduction to the Study of*
    International Relations (London: Macmillan, 1939), 119.

7   Hans Morgenthau, "The Machiavellian Utopia," *Ethics* 55, no. 2 (1945):
    145.

8   Hans Morgenthau, *Politics Among Nations: The Struggle for Power and*
    Peace (New York: Alfred A. Knopf, 1954), 12.

9   Morgenthau, *Politics Among Nations*, 13.

10 Thucydides, *The Peloponnesian War*, trans. Martin Hammond (Oxford:
    Oxford University Press, 2009), 302.

11 Thucydides, *Peloponnesian War*, 302.

12 Paul Alexander, *Machiavelli's Shadow: The Rise and Fall of Karl Rove* (New
    York: Rodale, 2008), 13.

13 Patrick Leahy, quoted in John Nichols, "Karl Rove: The Machiavelli Who
    Failed," *The Nation*, August 13, 2007, accessed December 28, 2014,
    http://www.thenation.com/blog/karl-rove-machiavelli-who-failed.

MODULE 11
IMPACT AND INFLUENCE TODAY

KEY POINTS

- *The Prince*, once criticized for its negative outlook, is now widely read for its realism and its emphasis on the importance of political effectiveness.

- One of Machiavelli's most important contributions in *The Prince* was his differentiation of "facts" and "values."* This distinction is used today by critics of totalitarianism.* They point out the hypocrisy of unjust regimes claiming to possess great virtue.

- The German philosopher Carl Schmitt* suggested that to maintain a strong state, citizens must believe their state is divinely given and that their enemies are shared and eternal.

Position

Niccolò Machiavelli's *The Prince* is relevant to contemporary politics because of its clear approach, its universal ideas and the insights it offers into political leadership. It deals with an essential question: what is the nature of power? It was among the first works to explore the notion of "realpolitik,"* which recognizes politics as a special domain, governed by the rules of power. Why is power so important? Because it is the only dependable way a political figure can control the world around him.

In 2013, the American political and sociological thinker Jared Diamond* was asked by the *New York Times*, "If you could require the President to read one book, what would it be?" His answer was, "*The*

> **❝Never mind how you are ... appear as you would like to be. ❞**
> Hannah Arendt, "From Machiavelli to Marx"

Prince. Machiavelli is frequently dismissed today as an amoral cynic, a man unconcerned by the notion of right and wrong who considers the end to justify the means. In fact, Machiavelli is a crystal-clear realist who understands the limits and uses of power."[1] Diamond points to the distinction Machiavelli draws not only between morality* and politics, but also between circumstances the shrewd politician can control (through "*virtù*")* and those no politician can control ("*fortuna*").*[2] *The Prince* is still important because the rules of power politics do not change.

Interaction

Machiavelli's work did not give rise to a defined school of thought. However, prominent political scientists, including American academics Allan Bloom* and Harvey Mansfield,* believe all modern political thought owes at least something to *The Prince*. Machiavelli can be seen as the first modern political thinker. But rather than presenting a political theory of its own, *The Prince* simply exposes the hypocrisy of any political system claiming to be based on morality.

Over 400 years after *The Prince* was first published, Machiavelli's ideas were used by the English novelist and thinker George Orwell.* In his novel *Nineteen Eighty Four* Orwell imagines a futuristic society that exercises total control over its citizens, while proclaiming virtues of justice and patriotism. It does so in the name of the absolute government of the ruler, "Big Brother:""...the songs, the processions, the banners, the hiking, the drilling with dummy rifles, the yelling of slogans, the worship of Big Brother—it was all a sort of glorious game."[3] Orwell makes it clear that the declaration that "Big Brother"

63

is just merely serves to promote the *injustice* of this abusive government.

The German-born political theorist Hannah Arendt* wrote about totalitarianism, the system of government that demands absolute obedience to the state. She agreed that Machiavelli laid bare the hypocrisy behind the ethical claims of the powerful. "Never mind how you are," Arendt interprets Machiavelli's advice, "appear as you would like to be."[4]

The Continuing Debate

Carl Schmitt* was a twentieth-century German jurist and political thinker who joined the Nazi Party* and was associated with the authoritarian* rise of Adolf Hitler.*[5] He offered a response to Machiavelli's "fact-value"* challenge. Schmitt wrote, "The concept of the state presupposes the concept of the political."[6] In other words, the very existence of a "state" shows that people were uniting on the basis of a shared political outlook. So Schmitt argues that politics is all about people going beyond their individual desires and living for ideology.

Schmitt believed that people are bound together by the idea that they have a collective identity that is defined by a collective enemy.[7] While liberal* thinkers—like Arendt—believe the most important distinction in politics is between facts and values (what is true versus what is believed), Schmitt believed the most important distinction is between friend and enemy (who "we" are versus who "they" are). Political systems are based on the personal and ideological bonds that arise from shared beliefs and a common enemy. It is beliefs, not facts, that constitute politics.

For Schmitt, Machiavelli's distinction between facts and values undermines the strength of the state. If citizens realize that their commitments to one another and their commitments to combat their enemies serve not their own needs, but the needs of the powerful, then the entire political community falls apart.

NOTES

1   Jared Diamond, "Jared Diamond: By the Book," *New York Times*, January 17, 2013, accessed December 14, 2014, http://www.nytimes.com/2013/01/20/books/review/jared-diamond-by-the-book.html?pagewanted=all.

2   Diamond, "By the Book."

3   George Orwell, *Nineteen Eighty Four* (London: Penguin Books, 2013), 23.

4   Hannah Arendt, "From Machiavelli to Marx," in *The Hannah Arendt Papers* (Washington: Library of Congress, 1965), 5.

5   Jan-Werner Müller, *A Dangerous Mind: Carl Schmitt in Post-War European Thought* (New Haven: Yale University Press, 2003), 2.

6   Carl Schmitt, *The Concept of the Political* (Chicago: University of Chicago Press, 2007), 1.

7   Schmitt, *Concept*, 25.

MODULE 12
WHERE NEXT?

KEY POINTS

- *The Prince's* unflinching honesty will continue to be important, especially in the realm of politics.

- Machiavelli's view that leaders must act effectively and decisively to protect the state can still be seen today, for example in the actions of US President Barack Obama* against his opponent Osama bin Laden.*

- *The Prince* remains important because of Machiavelli's timeless insight into the true nature of political rule.

Potential

Niccolò Machiavelli's *The Prince* is not in line with traditional political philosophy. Machiavelli did not advance an agenda for others to follow. Instead, his work exposes the moral claims underpinning any political system. In this, Machiavelli can be compared with the nineteenth-century German philosopher Friedrich Nietzsche.* In his masterworks, *Thus Spake Zarathustra* and *The Will to Power*, Nietzsche, like Machiavelli, was consciously "anti-system." Both men sought to differentiate themselves from contemporary or mainstream schools of thought.

In *Zarathustra*, Nietzsche imagines that Zarathustra, a great man himself, comes down from a mountain to teach men of greatness. He comes across a saint who encourages him to lead a simple, contemplative life in service of God. Zarathustra says to himself: "Could it be possible! This old saint in the forest hath not yet heard of it, that God is dead!"[1] The great man—the object of Nietzsche's theory—realizes that God, representing any traditional source of

> **❝** So if we return to the Situation Room and to the decisions presidents make there, Machiavelli's *The Prince* tells us the question is not whether one human being should have the right to make such terrifying determinations. The essence of power, even in a democracy, is to use violence to protect the republic. **❞**
>
> Michael Ignatieff, "Machiavelli Was Right"

morality,* has faded from relevance.

"Machiavellianism,"* Nietzsche argues, "is superhuman, divine, transcendental," because it frees humanity from the shackles of false morality. "Freedom from morality," or the morality imposed by others, "for the sake of the domination of virtue—that is the canon."[2] Nietzsche believes virtue is something invented by great men to impose their greatness on lesser men—to subscribe to conventional virtue is to accept one's status as a slave rather than a master. Nietzsche also draws the same distinction that Machiavelli draws—between *virtù** (power, effectiveness, and forcefulness), and virtue, (traditional morality).[3] As long as there are establishments to be criticized the works of Machiavelli and Nietzsche will continue to challenge them.

Future Directions

Machiavelli's approach to politics remains relevant beyond the world of theory. The British political theorist Alan Ryan* writes, "… the staying power of *The Prince* comes from … its insistence on the need for a clear-sighted appreciation of how men really are distinct from the moralizing [nonsense] about how they ought to be."[4]

The Canadian academic Michael Ignatieff* cites Ryan and relates Machiavellian insight to the foreign policy of US President Barack Obama. He points to the moment when the United States found and killed the Saudi Arabian militant Osama bin Laden. "If we return,"

Ignatieff writes, "to the Situation Room and the decisions Presidents make there, Machiavelli's *The Prince* tells us the question is not whether one human being should have the right to make such terrifying determinations" over life and death, but rather, how best to do what is necessary to "protect the republic."[5] Machiavelli's message is that leaders need to act effectively to ensure the survival of the state. This will continue to inform policy as long as politics remains a contest among the powerful.

Machiavelli uncovers the naked truth of the assassination of bin Laden. It can be dressed up as justice, but it remains the taking of a human life by a liberal* republic. Machiavelli would not say this is wrong; he merely challenges his readers to recognize that drastic action must be taken when necessary. Dressing it up in the cloak of morality is a necessary falsehood.

Summary

"Anyone who picks up Machiavelli's *The Prince*," writes the American academic Harvey Mansfield,* "holds in his hands the most famous book on politics ever written."[6] He goes on: "We cannot ... agree that *The Prince* is the most famous book on politics without immediately correcting this to say that it is the most infamous."[7] This is perhaps the best summary of *The Prince* and its relationship to political thought. It is famous as a force for tearing down weak, ethical rules and their equally weak claim to political relevance. It is infamous for its bold recognition of the reality of evil.

The French author Victor Hugo* discusses Machiavelli and *The Prince*'s impact in his book, *Les Misérables*. "Machiavelli is not an evil genius," Hugo writes, "nor a demon, nor a cowardly and miserable writer; he is nothing but the fact."[8] Machiavelli's overarching concern was not "what would we *like* to work?" It was a simpler question, "What works?" In his chapter on avoiding flatterers, Machiavelli reminds princes: "there is no other way to guard yourself against flattery than by making men understand that by telling you the truth they will not injure you."[9] Moral manuals praising princes as ethical heroes may be lovely to read, but the truth—which is what Machiavelli really offers—is worth infinitely more.

NOTES

1   Friedrich Nietzsche, *Thus Spake Zarathustra* (New York: Macmillan, 1911), 3.

2   Friedrich Nietzsche, *The Will to Power* (New York: Random House, 1968), 171.

3   Nietzsche, *Will to Power*, 176.

4   Alan Ryan, *On Machiavelli: The Search for Glory* (W. W. Norton & Company: New York, 2012), 51–52.

5   Michael Ignatieff, "Machiavelli Was Right," *The Atlantic*, December 2013, accessed December 28, 2014, http://www.theatlantic.com/magazine/archive/2013/12/machiavelli-was-right/354672/?single_page=true.

6   Harvey C. Mansfield, introduction to *The Prince* by Niccolò Machiavelli (Chicago: University of Chicago Press, 1998), vii.

7   Mansfield, introduction, vii.

8   Victor Hugo, *Les Misérables*, trans. Douglas Crawford (New York: Macmillan, 1915), 247.

9   Machiavelli, *The Prince* (Chicago: University of Chicago Press, 1998), 81.

GLOSSARY

GLOSSARY OF TERMS

Aristocracy: the ruling or upper class of society; the aristocracy is generally made up of those with hereditary titles

Authoritarian: a system of social organization—usually associated with military rule or a police state—where obedience to authority (in the form of the central government) is enforced.

Classical era: a period of Eurasian history from the fifth century B.C.E. to the fifth century C.E. that was dominated by Greece and Rome. It also often refers (implicitly) to an idealized version of life in these states.

Early modern period: a historical period in Europe that lasted from the fifteenth to the eighteenth centuries, and is generally defined as starting with the fall of Constantinople in 1453 and ending with the beginning of democratic revolution in France in 1789.

Enlightenment: the name given to the period of European history from the mid-seventeenth to the late eighteenth century. It is often considered to be the period when liberal politics and the scientific method were born, and it prompted the discarding of many traditional ways of life.

Fact-value distinction: a concept separating what is (facts) from what ought to be (values). This is the difference between "there is a road outside my house" and "there should be a road outside my house."

Fortuna: fortune or fate.

French Wars of Religion: the name given to a period of civil strife in France that lasted from 1562 to 1598 between factions associated with the Protestant "Huguenots" and Roman Catholics. The wars claimed between two and four million lives.

House of Medici: a Florentine banking family and political dynasty that had influence between the fifteenth and the eighteenth centuries. They rose from common roots by opening one of the world's first banks and went on to rule large parts of Italy.

Huguenots: a group of French Protestants who endured much official persecution at the hands of the Roman Catholic French state, especially in the seventeenth century.

Humanism: a school of thought that arose in Renaissance Italy. One of the key points of humanism was the study of ancient texts, rather than exclusively the Bible, to gain wisdom.

International relations: the study of politics in the international sphere, focusing on what is distinctive about the international as opposed to the domestic.

Liberalism: a political philosophy that emphasizes the importance of individual liberty and welfare.

Machiavellianism: a term derived from "Machiavelli" to describe the use of cunning and deceitfulness, particularly in order to hold on to power.

Medieval period: the name given to a period of European history between the fifth and the fifteenth centuries. The fall of the Roman Empire in the fifth century led to a patchwork of kingdoms springing up across Western Europe. It is believed that the medieval period was a "dark age" where little cultural advancement took place, but this is not universally agreed.

Mirrors for princes: a style of writing from early modern Europe which gives accounts of political life emphasizing how rulers should rule, and what the ideal ruler should be like.

Morality: a system of rule-based values defining people's conduct with one another.

Nazi Party: Short for "National Socialist Worker's Party," this was a political movement in Germany, active from the 1920s to the 1940s. The Nazis pursued a totalitarian domestic policy and an aggressive foreign policy that led to World War II.

Necessita: willingness to do what is necessary, regardless of the morality (or lack of) of the actions.

Papal Index: a list of books that were officially banned by the Roman Catholic Church. The Index ceased to exist in 1966.

Raison d'état: literally, the "reason of state"; a political term referring to the national interest.

Realism: a school of international relations theory that assumes: (1) states are the primary actors; (2) states all share the goal of survival; (3) states provide for their own security.

Realpolitik: the practice of politics based exclusively on reality, rather than ideological factors.

Renaissance: the name given to a period of European history between the fourteenth and seventeenth centuries, characterized by rapid progression in art, science, and technology.

Republic of Florence: the democratic government of Florence, founded in 1115, that turned into a hereditary dukedom in 1533.

Rhetoric: the art of persuasive communication.

Roman Catholicism: a branch of the Christian faith with a rigid hierarchy, from the Pope in the Vatican City, down to priests in individual parishes around the world. It defined social life and political organization in Europe until the emergence of Protestantism as an alternative in 1517.

Satire: the use of humor or ridicule to expose something that is wrong in the world (especially with relation to politics or social life) as ridiculous or wrongheaded.

Scorched earth: a military strategy involving complete destruction of a given territory. Its everyday use indicates a ruthless approach to solving a problem.

Social contract theory: an approach to political philosophy that argues that society arises from an agreement between people (a contract) to create the first structures that define their relationships with one another.

Sovereignty: refers to the complete authority of a state to govern a given area.

Teleology: a way of looking at the world focusing on ideal end states.

The best example is the idea that every acorn has a "telos" in it of being an oak tree.

Totalitarian: a form of government or social organization where the state takes complete and brutal control of every aspect of life.

Utopia: a term coined by Sir Thomas More in his 1516 book of the same name, referring to the ideal state or place in terms of laws, society and government.

Virtù: a term used by Machiavelli to refer to the qualities of courage and skillfulness as distinct from morality.

PEOPLE MENTIONED IN THE TEXT

Agathocles (361–289 b.c.e.) was the Greek tyrant of Syracuse and King of Sicily. He was a commoner (the son of a potter) who rose to power through brutality and violence.

Paul Alexander is an American reporter. He is a political biographer of many right-wing American figures, including Karl Rove and John McCain.

Hannah Arendt (1906–75) was a German Jewish philosopher. She was most concerned with the nature and use of power, and the ways in which political systems become authoritarian or totalitarian.

Aristotle (384–322 b.c.e.) was a Greek philosopher and tutor to Alexander the Great. His book, *Politics*, investigates political "ideals," asking whether or not politics is natural, who the best rulers and citizens are, and what the ideal political constitution is.

Saint Augustine of Hippo (c.e. 354–430) was an early Christian political theorist from North Africa. He believed the concept of "grace" (essentially the idea that God has the ability to absolve any sin) will elevate human politics to a more divinely perfect "city of God."

Francis Bacon (1561–1626) was an English philosopher and statesman. He believed that truth needed to be established through looking at evidence from the real world.

Kenneth Bartlett is a Canadian historian of the Renaissance. One of his primary interests is the transition of the West from the medieval period to the Renaissance period.

Osama bin Laden (1957–2011) was a Saudi Arabian militant, former leader of al-Qaeda, and one of the main architects of 9/11, the September 11, 2001 terrorist attacks on the World Trade Center. He was killed in 2011.

Isaiah Berlin (1909–97) was a Russian British philosopher and political thinker. His most famous work was on the concept of liberty, drawing a line between "negative liberty" (what we are free to do without interference) and "positive liberty" (what we are enabled to do with help).

Otto von Bismarck (1815–98) was a nineteenth-century Prussian statesman. He is considered to be the founder of modern Germany, and was the first Chancellor of Germany.

Allan Bloom (1930–92) was an American political thinker and philosopher. He was primarily concerned with bringing insights from ancient philosophers, especially Plato, into modern life.

Napoleon Bonaparte (1769–1821) was a French political figure who rose to prominence through the early nineteenth century to become Emperor of France from 1804 to 1815. He led the French army across continental Europe, invading countries from Spain to Russia.

Cesare Borgia (1475–1507) was an Italian nobleman and *condottiero* (meaning mercenary warlord). Also known as the Duke of Valentinois, he was a ruthless politician, responsible for conquering and subduing entire regions of Italy.

George W. Bush (b. 1946) is an American politician and former president of the United States, in office from 2001 to 2009. He famously presided over the "War on Terror," which saw the beginning of American involvement in wars in Iraq and Afghanistan.

Edward Hallett (E. H.) Carr (1892–1982) was an English diplomat and political writer. He was famously cynical about the possibility of peace in international relations, but also made key contributions to the study of history.

Baldassare Castiglione (1478–1529) was an Italian court figure and political thinker. *The Book of the Courtier* is his most famous work, written about the beauty and wonder of the life of the nobility.

Richard Christie is an American psychologist who, along with Florence Geis, devised the "Mach" test, a 20-question survey to determine the subject's "level" of Machiavellianism.

Marcus Tullius Cicero (106–43 b.c.e.) was a Roman politician and political thinker. He is as famous for his political career, in which he was an opponent of Julius Caesar and an advocate for republican government, as he is for his political thought, in which he laid out the obligations of those who aimed to govern well.

Bernard Crick (1929–2008) was a British political theorist. He famously wrote books including *In Defence of Politics*, which argues that power struggles in the political arena provide a substitute for force and coercion.

Jared Diamond (b. 1937) is an American geographer and political thinker. He is famous for his theory that the geographies of different lands will go a long way to shape the culture and fate of those who occupy them.

Frederick II, also called Frederick the Great, (1712–86) was King of Prussia from 1740 to 1786. His rule marked a key turning point in the modernization of Prussia, including the professionalization of the military and the creation of a bureaucratic system of administration.

Florence Geis (1933–93) was an American psychologist who, in addition to working on Machiavellianism with Richard Christie, was primarily interested in the role of sex and gender in psychology.

Alberico Gentili (1552–1608) was an Italian legal thinker who was famous as professor of civil law at the University of Oxford. He was among the first to write about international law, and advised the English government on its foreign policy.

Innocent Gentillet (1535–88) was a French lawyer and political thinker. He belonged to the "Huguenots," a religious minority in France that suffered persecution in his lifetime.

Allan Gilbert (1888–1976) was an American historian. His book *Machiavelli's Prince and its Forerunners* seats Machiavelli in the intellectual history of political advice, looking at sources as famous as Thomas Aquinas, but also at lesser-known Renaissance thinkers such as Patrizi.

Felix Gilbert (1905–91) was a German American historian. While he had a variety of interests, his work on the Renaissance attempts to discern a "Renaissance" style of political theory.

G. W. F. (Georg Wilhelm Friedrich) Hegel (1770–1831) was a German philosopher who focused on the role of ideas—in terms of a desire for freedom—in the progression of history.

Adolf Hitler (1889–1945) was the Chancellor of Germany from 1933 until his death in 1945. Hitler's Nazi party pursued a policy of aggressive nationalism, racism, and totalitarianism, ultimately leading to the outbreak of World War II in 1939.

Thomas Hobbes (1588–1679) was an English political thinker. His most famous book, *Leviathan*, argued that a strong state was necessary in order to protect the interests of the governed.

Robert Howse is a Canadian professor of law and philosophy. He is interested in re-reading the conflict between Leo Strauss and Carl Schmitt on political violence and ideology.

Victor Hugo (1802–85) was a celebrated French writer. Perhaps his most famous novel is *Les Misérables*.

Michael Ignatieff (b. 1947) is a Canadian international relations thinker and politician. His political thought is, among other things, concerned with the concept of humanitarian intervention.

Louis XII (1462–1515) was King of France from 1498 to 1515, during which time he had large territorial holdings in Italy. In the "Italian Wars," Louis XII fought to extend his influence over Italy and brought large parts of the country under his control.

Vladimir Lenin (1870–1924) was a Russian revolutionary figure and first Chairman of the Soviet Union. Under his ideology, all private property in Russia was confiscated, the old ruling class was overturned, and Communism was implemented.

Titus Livius (Livy) (59/64 b.c.e.– c.e.17) was a Roman historian, whose history of Rome (entitled *Ab Urbe Condita Libri*, or *Books from* *the Foundation of the City*) is the main source for the earliest legends of Rome's founding.

John Locke (1632–1704) was an English political thinker, strongly associated with the liberal tradition and social contract theory. He believed that societies of laws arose in order to protect individual liberty and secure private property, enabling the greater welfare of all.

Harvey Mansfield (b. 1932) is an American professor of government. In general, he takes a relatively conservative approach to theory. Most of his books discuss thinkers from Socrates to Edmund Burke.

Friedrich Meinecke (1862–1954) was a German historian. While he is a controversial figure because of his association with the Nazi Party, his "nationalist" history of Germany provides an important distinction between state power and ethics.

Thomas More (1478–1535) was a lawyer, philosopher and statesman, who rose to the position of Lord Chancellor in the court of Henry VIII of England. His *Utopia* describes the ideal state in terms of laws, society and government.

Hans Morgenthau (1904–80) was a German American political thinker and international relations academic. His *Politics Among Nations* was one of the first modern, systematic studies of international power politics.

Benito Mussolini (1883–1945) was prime minister of Italy from 1922 until 1943. He was a key figure in the creation of "fascism," which valued ultra-nationalism, militarism, and expansion of national industry at all costs.

John Nichols (b. 1959) is an American journalist. He is a regular contributor to left-wing publications, including *The Nation* and *The Progressive*.

Friedrich Nietzsche (1844–1900) was a German philosopher. He was famous for his idea of the "ubermensch," or "over-man," the force of whose will would enable him to rise above social control. He was most concerned with "life affirmation," which rejected the idea that moral goodness was found in submission and death, and instead encouraged domination in life.

Barack Obama (b. 1961) is an American politician and president of the United States, who took office in 2009 and again in 2013, presiding over some difficult periods of American history, including the bailout of the financial sector after the crisis of 2007 and the end of the "War on Terror."

George Orwell (1903–50) was an English journalist and satirist. He is best known for his book *Nineteen Eighty Four*, which painted a picture of a totalitarian world.

Francesco Patrizi (1529–97) was an Italian philosopher. While he wrote a work in the "mirror for princes" style, he was more known as a scientist and theologian.

Otto Pflanze (1918–2007) was a historian of nineteenth-century Germany. Best known as the leading biographer of Bismarck, Pflanze also focused on the social and intellectual forces that shaped the birth of Germany.

Plato (429–347 b.c.e.) was a Greek philosopher, often considered to be among the most famous philosophers ever. "Platonism" is a theory of ideals, stating that abstract ideas of perfect things exist, and that existing things are pale reflections of these abstract ideas. *The Republic* was Plato's effort to imagine a perfectly just state.

John Roe is an English professor of Renaissance literature. His primary interest is in Shakespeare, and in the comparison of Italian and English Renaissance literature, as well as American poetry.

Romulus (seventh century b.c.e.) was the legendary founder of Rome along with his twin brother, Remus. He gave the city its laws, its senate, and its legions—but he also famously murdered Remus at the moment of Rome's founding.

Jean-Jacques Rousseau (1712–78) was a Genevan philosopher associated with the Enlightenment. His theories deal with the nature of property and inequality.

Karl Rove (b. 1950) is an American political strategist who was close to President George W. Bush during his period in office.

Alan Ryan (b. 1940) is a British political theorist and professor of politics at the University of Oxford. Ryan looks at the development of modern liberalism from early-modern roots, especially relating to John Stuart Mill.

Girolamo Savonarola (1452–98) was an Italian religious figure turned political leader. In 1494, he seized control of Florence and famously burned all art, furniture, and other pleasurable things in order to make the city more devout.

Carl Schmitt (1888–1985) was a German philosopher and legal theorist. His work *Political Theology* influentially argued that political concepts are just religious concepts minus God: they are believed through faith, and inspire fierce loyalty in those who follow them. His association with Nazism has led to much controversy surrounding his thought.

William Shakespeare (1564–1616) was an English playwright and poet, and is considered by many to be the greatest writer in the English language.

Quentin Skinner (b. 1940) is a British historian of early modern Europe. Skinner argues for the importance of the idea of "republicanism" in history, and believes this idea provides legitimacy to modern society.

Socrates (470/469–399 b.c.e.) was a Greek philosopher, and the teacher of Plato. Socrates was often used as the main character in Plato's writing, which was presented as dialogues between Socrates and others. No writing directly attributable to him survives.

Piero di Tommaso Soderini (1452–1522) was a Florentine statesman who was elected to become the city-state's *gonfalonier* (head of the civil administration) for life in 1502.

Leo Strauss (1899–1973) was a German political thinker notable for his study of classical political philosophy. He was among the first twentieth-century thinkers to make a serious attempt at reviving Machiavelli, and to look at him as the first modern political thinker. Strauss was nonetheless critical of Machiavelli's amorality.

Thucydides (460–395 b.c.e.) was a Greek historian and military leader. His *History of the Peloponnesian War* is widely considered to be the first "realist" text, as it laid bare the logic of "might is right."

Miles Unger is an American historian of Renaissance Italy, especially Florence. In addition to Machiavelli, he has written books on Michelangelo and Magnifico.

Maurizio Viroli (b. 1952) is an Italian historian. He specializes in the study and re-reading of Machiavelli in his historical context.

WORKS CITED

WORKS CITED

Alexander, Paul. *Machiavelli's Shadow: The Rise and Fall of Karl Rove*. New York: Rodale, 2008.

Arditti, Michael. "Machiavelli's Dangerous Book for Men." *Telegraph*, January 19, 2008. Accessed December 12, 2014. http://www.telegraph.co.uk/culture/books/non_fictionreviews/3670598/Machiavellis-dangerous-book-for-men.html.

Arendt, Hannah. "From Machiavelli to Marx." In *The Hannah Arendt Papers*. Washington: Library of Congress, 1965.

Bartlett, Kenneth. "Introduction to the Italian Renaissance." In *The Civilization of the Italian Renaissance: A Sourcebook*, edited by Kenneth Bartlett, 1–13. Toronto: University of Toronto Press, 2011.

Berlin, Isaiah. "The Originality of Machiavelli." In *Against the Current: Essays in the History of Ideas*. Princeton: Princeton University Press, 2013.

Berlin, Isaiah. "A Special Supplement: The Question of Machiavelli." *New York Review of Books*, November 4, 1971. Accessed December 11, 2014. http://www.nybooks.com/articles/archives/1971/nov/04/a-special-supplement-the-question-of-machiavelli/.

Bismarck, Otto. "Blood and Iron Speech." Accessed December 14, 2014. http://germanhistorydocs.ghi-dc.org/sub_document.cfm?document_id=250.

Bloom, Allan. *Closing of the American Mind*. New York: Simon and Schuster, 1987.

Carr, E. H. *The Twenty Years' Crisis: An Introduction to the Study of International Relations*. London: Macmillan, 1939.

Christie, Richard, and Florence Geis. *Studies in Machiavellianism*. New York: Academic Press, 1970.

Coby, Patrick. *Machiavelli's Romans: Liberty and Greatness in the Discourses on Livy*. Oxford: Lexington Books, 1999.

Devereaux, Daniel. "Classical Political Philosophy: Plato and Aristotle." In *The Oxford Handbook of the History of Political Philosophy*, edited by George Klosko, 96–120. Oxford: Oxford University Press, 2011.

Diamond, Jared. "Jared Diamond: By the Book." *New York Times*, January 17, 2013. Accessed December 14, 2014. http://www.nytimes.com/2013/01/20/books/review/jared-diamond-by-the-book.html?pagewanted=all.

Gilbert, Allan. *Machiavelli's Prince and its Forerunners*. Durham: Duke University Press, 1938.

Gilbert, Felix. "The Concept of Nationalism in Machiavelli's Prince." *Studies in the Renaissance* 1 (1954): 38–48.

Hegel, G. W. F. *The German Constitution*. Accessed December 14, 2014. https://www.marxists.org/reference/archive/hegel/works/gc/ch02.htm.

Hobbes, Thomas. *Leviathan*. Digireads Classics, 2009.

Howse, Robert. *Leo Strauss: Man of Peace*. Cambridge: Cambridge University Press, 2014.

Ignatieff, Michael. "Machiavelli Was Right." *The Atlantic*, December 2013. Accessed December 28, 2014. http://www.theatlantic.com/magazine/archive/2013/12/machiavelli-was-right/354672/?single_page=true.

Kahn, Victoria. "Machiavelli's Afterlife and Reputation to the Eighteenth Century." In *The Cambridge Companion to Machiavelli*, edited by John M. Najemy, 239–256. Cambridge: Cambridge University Press, 2010.

Klosko, George. *History of Political Theory: An Introduction: Volume II: Modern*. Oxford: Oxford University Press, 2013.

Lambertini, Roberto. "Mirrors for Princes." In *Encyclopedia of Medieval Philosophy: Philosophy Between 500 and 1500*, edited by Henrik Lagerlund, 791–7. Amsterdam: Springer Netherlands, 2011.

Livy. *The Rise of Rome: Books 1–5*. Translated by T. J. Luce. Oxford: Oxford University Press, 1998.

Lovett, Frank. "The Path of the Courtier: Castiglione, Machiavelli, and the Loss of Republican Liberty." *Review of Politics* 74 (2012): 589–605.

Luvaas, Jay. *Frederick the Great on the Art of War*. New York: The Free Press, 1999.

Machiavelli, Niccolò. *The Discourses*. London: Penguin Books, 1970.

The Prince. London: Penguin Books, 2003.

The Prince. Chicago: University of Chicago Press, 1998.

The Prince. Oxford: Oxford World's Classics, 2005.

Mansfield, Harvey C. "Machiavelli's Political Science." *The American Political Science Review* 75, no. 2 (1981):293–305.

Meinecke, Friedrich. *Machiavellism: The Doctrine of Raison d'État and its Place in Modern History*. New Brunswick: Transaction Publishers, 1998.

Nichols, John. "Karl Rove: The Machiavelli Who Failed." *The Nation*, August 13, 2007. Accessed December 28, 2014. http://www.thenation.com/blog/karl-rove-machiavelli-who-failed.

Nietzsche, Friedrich. *Thus Spake Zarathustra*. New York: Macmillan, 1911.

Orwell, George. *Nineteen Eighty Four*. London: Penguin Books, 2013.

Pangle, Thomas L., and Timothy W. Burns. *The Key Texts of Political Philosophy: An Introduction*. Cambridge: University of Cambridge Press, 2015.

Pflanze, Otto. "Bismarck's Realpolitik." *The Review of Politics* 20, no. 4 (1958): 492–514.

Plato. *The Republic*. Translated by R. E. Allen. New Haven: Yale University Press, 2006.

Roe, John Allan. *Shakespeare and Machiavelli*. Cambridge: D. S. Brewer, 2002.

Rousseau, Jean-Jacques. *The Social Contract*. New York: Cosimo, 2008.

Ryan, Alan. *On Machiavelli: The Search for Glory*. W. W. Norton & Company: New York, 2012.

Saint Augustine of Hippo. *The City of God*. Edinburgh: T. & T. Clark, 1841.

Schmitt, Carl. *The Concept of the Political*. Chicago: University of Chicago Press, 2007.

Strauss, Leo. "Machiavelli's Intention: *The Prince*." *The American Political Science Review* 51, no. 1 (1957): 13–40.

Strauss, Leo. Introduction to *History of Political Philosophy*, edited by Leo Strauss and Joseph Cropsey, 1–7. Chicago: University of Chicago Press, 1987.

Thucydides. *The Peloponnesian War*. Translated by Martin Hammond. Oxford: Oxford University Press, 2009.

Truman, Ronald W. *Spanish Treatises on Government, Society and Religion in the Time of Philip II*. Leiden: Koninkijke Brill NV, 1999.

Unger, Miles. *Machiavelli: A Biography*. New York: Simon and Schuster, 2011.

Warburton, Nigel, Jon Pike and Derek Matravers. *Reading Political Philosophy: Machiavelli to Mill*. Abingdon: Routledge, 2006.

Werner-Müller, Jan. *A Dangerous Mind: Carl Schmitt in Post-War European Thought*. New Haven: Yale University Press, 2003.

THE MACAT LIBRARY
BY DISCIPLINE

AFRICANA STUDIES

Chinua Achebe's *An Image of Africa: Racism in Conrad's Heart of Darkness*
W. E. B. Du Bois's *The Souls of Black Folk*
Zora Neale Huston's *Characteristics of Negro Expression*
Martin Luther King Jr's *Why We Can't Wait*
Toni Morrison's *Playing in the Dark: Whiteness in the American Literary Imagination*

ANTHROPOLOGY

Arjun Appadurai's *Modernity at Large: Cultural Dimensions of Globalisation*
Philippe Ariès's *Centuries of Childhood*
Franz Boas's *Race, Language and Culture*
Kim Chan & Renée Mauborgne's *Blue Ocean Strategy*
Jared Diamond's *Guns, Germs & Steel: the Fate of Human Societies*
Jared Diamond's *Collapse: How Societies Choose to Fail or Survive*
E. E. Evans-Pritchard's *Witchcraft, Oracles and Magic Among the Azande*
James Ferguson's *The Anti-Politics Machine*
Clifford Geertz's *The Interpretation of Cultures*
David Graeber's *Debt: the First 5000 Years*
Karen Ho's *Liquidated: An Ethnography of Wall Street*
Geert Hofstede's *Culture's Consequences: Comparing Values, Behaviors, Institutes and Organizations across Nations*
Claude Lévi-Strauss's *Structural Anthropology*
Jay Macleod's *Ain't No Makin' It: Aspirations and Attainment in a Low-Income Neighborhood*
Saba Mahmood's *The Politics of Piety: The Islamic Revival and the Feminist Subject*
Marcel Mauss's *The Gift*

BUSINESS

Jean Lave & Etienne Wenger's *Situated Learning*
Theodore Levitt's *Marketing Myopia*
Burton G. Malkiel's *A Random Walk Down Wall Street*
Douglas McGregor's *The Human Side of Enterprise*
Michael Porter's *Competitive Strategy: Creating and Sustaining Superior Performance*
John Kotter's *Leading Change*
C. K. Prahalad & Gary Hamel's *The Core Competence of the Corporation*

CRIMINOLOGY

Michelle Alexander's *The New Jim Crow: Mass Incarceration in the Age of Colorblindness*
Michael R. Gottfredson & Travis Hirschi's *A General Theory of Crime*
Richard Herrnstein & Charles A. Murray's *The Bell Curve: Intelligence and Class Structure in American Life*
Elizabeth Loftus's *Eyewitness Testimony*
Jay Macleod's *Ain't No Makin' It: Aspirations and Attainment in a Low-Income Neighborhood*
Philip Zimbardo's *The Lucifer Effect*

ECONOMICS

Janet Abu-Lughod's *Before European Hegemony*
Ha-Joon Chang's *Kicking Away the Ladder*
David Brion Davis's *The Problem of Slavery in the Age of Revolution*
Milton Friedman's *The Role of Monetary Policy*
Milton Friedman's *Capitalism and Freedom*
David Graeber's *Debt: the First 5000 Years*
Friedrich Hayek's *The Road to Serfdom*
Karen Ho's *Liquidated: An Ethnography of Wall Street*

John Maynard Keynes's *The General Theory of Employment, Interest and Money*
Charles P. Kindleberger's *Manias, Panics and Crashes*
Robert Lucas's *Why Doesn't Capital Flow from Rich to Poor Countries?*
Burton G. Malkiel's *A Random Walk Down Wall Street*
Thomas Robert Malthus's *An Essay on the Principle of Population*
Karl Marx's *Capital*
Thomas Piketty's *Capital in the Twenty-First Century*
Amartya Sen's *Development as Freedom*
Adam Smith's *The Wealth of Nations*
Nassim Nicholas Taleb's *The Black Swan: The Impact of the Highly Improbable*
Amos Tversky's & Daniel Kahneman's *Judgment under Uncertainty: Heuristics and Biases*
Mahbub Ul Haq's *Reflections on Human Development*
Max Weber's *The Protestant Ethic and the Spirit of Capitalism*

FEMINISM AND GENDER STUDIES

Judith Butler's *Gender Trouble*
Simone De Beauvoir's *The Second Sex*
Michel Foucault's *History of Sexuality*
Betty Friedan's *The Feminine Mystique*
Saba Mahmood's *The Politics of Piety: The Islamic Revival and the Feminist Subject*
Joan Wallach Scott's *Gender and the Politics of History*
Mary Wollstonecraft's *A Vindication of the Rights of Women*
Virginia Woolf's *A Room of One's Own*

GEOGRAPHY

The Brundtland Report's *Our Common Future*
Rachel Carson's *Silent Spring*
Charles Darwin's *On the Origin of Species*
James Ferguson's *The Anti-Politics Machine*
Jane Jacobs's *The Death and Life of Great American Cities*
James Lovelock's *Gaia: A New Look at Life on Earth*
Amartya Sen's *Development as Freedom*
Mathis Wackernagel & William Rees's *Our Ecological Footprint*

HISTORY

Janet Abu-Lughod's *Before European Hegemony*
Benedict Anderson's *Imagined Communities*
Bernard Bailyn's *The Ideological Origins of the American Revolution*
Hanna Batatu's *The Old Social Classes And The Revolutionary Movements Of Iraq*
Christopher Browning's *Ordinary Men: Reserve Police Batallion 101 and the Final Solution in Poland*
Edmund Burke's *Reflections on the Revolution in France*
William Cronon's *Nature's Metropolis: Chicago And The Great West*
Alfred W. Crosby's *The Columbian Exchange*
Hamid Dabashi's *Iran: A People Interrupted*
David Brion Davis's *The Problem of Slavery in the Age of Revolution*
Nathalie Zemon Davis's *The Return of Martin Guerre*
Jared Diamond's *Guns, Germs & Steel: the Fate of Human Societies*
Frank Dikotter's *Mao's Great Famine*
John W Dower's *War Without Mercy: Race And Power In The Pacific War*
W. E. B. Du Bois's *The Souls of Black Folk*
Richard J. Evans's *In Defence of History*
Lucien Febvre's *The Problem of Unbelief in the 16th Century*
Sheila Fitzpatrick's *Everyday Stalinism*

Eric Foner's *Reconstruction: America's Unfinished Revolution, 1863-1877*
Michel Foucault's *Discipline and Punish*
Michel Foucault's *History of Sexuality*
Francis Fukuyama's *The End of History and the Last Man*
John Lewis Gaddis's *We Now Know: Rethinking Cold War History*
Ernest Gellner's *Nations and Nationalism*
Eugene Genovese's *Roll, Jordan, Roll: The World the Slaves Made*
Carlo Ginzburg's *The Night Battles*
Daniel Goldhagen's *Hitler's Willing Executioners*
Jack Goldstone's *Revolution and Rebellion in the Early Modern World*
Antonio Gramsci's *The Prison Notebooks*
Alexander Hamilton, John Jay & James Madison's *The Federalist Papers*
Christopher Hill's *The World Turned Upside Down*
Carole Hillenbrand's *The Crusades: Islamic Perspectives*
Thomas Hobbes's *Leviathan*
Eric Hobsbawm's *The Age Of Revolution*
John A. Hobson's *Imperialism: A Study*
Albert Hourani's *History of the Arab Peoples*
Samuel P. Huntington's *The Clash of Civilizations and the Remaking of World Order*
C. L. R. James's *The Black Jacobins*
Tony Judt's *Postwar: A History of Europe Since 1945*
Ernst Kantorowicz's *The King's Two Bodies: A Study in Medieval Political Theology*
Paul Kennedy's *The Rise and Fall of the Great Powers*
Ian Kershaw's *The "Hitler Myth": Image and Reality in the Third Reich*
John Maynard Keynes's *The General Theory of Employment, Interest and Money*
Charles P. Kindleberger's *Manias, Panics and Crashes*
Martin Luther King Jr's *Why We Can't Wait*
Henry Kissinger's *World Order: Reflections on the Character of Nations and the Course of History*
Thomas Kuhn's *The Structure of Scientific Revolutions*
Georges Lefebvre's *The Coming of the French Revolution*
John Locke's *Two Treatises of Government*
Niccolò Machiavelli's *The Prince*
Thomas Robert Malthus's *An Essay on the Principle of Population*
Mahmood Mamdani's *Citizen and Subject: Contemporary Africa And The Legacy Of Late Colonialism*
Karl Marx's *Capital*
Stanley Milgram's *Obedience to Authority*
John Stuart Mill's *On Liberty*
Thomas Paine's *Common Sense*
Thomas Paine's *Rights of Man*
Geoffrey Parker's *Global Crisis: War, Climate Change and Catastrophe in the Seventeenth Century*
Jonathan Riley-Smith's *The First Crusade and the Idea of Crusading*
Jean-Jacques Rousseau's *The Social Contract*
Joan Wallach Scott's *Gender and the Politics of History*
Theda Skocpol's *States and Social Revolutions*
Adam Smith's *The Wealth of Nations*
Timothy Snyder's *Bloodlands: Europe Between Hitler and Stalin*
Sun Tzu's *The Art of War*
Keith Thomas's *Religion and the Decline of Magic*
Thucydides's *The History of the Peloponnesian War*
Frederick Jackson Turner's *The Significance of the Frontier in American History*
Odd Arne Westad's *The Global Cold War: Third World Interventions And The Making Of Our Times*

The Macat Library By Discipline

LITERATURE

Chinua Achebe's *An Image of Africa: Racism in Conrad's Heart of Darkness*
Roland Barthes's *Mythologies*
Homi K. Bhabha's *The Location of Culture*
Judith Butler's *Gender Trouble*
Simone De Beauvoir's *The Second Sex*
Ferdinand De Saussure's *Course in General Linguistics*
T. S. Eliot's *The Sacred Wood: Essays on Poetry and Criticism*
Zora Neale Huston's *Characteristics of Negro Expression*
Toni Morrison's *Playing in the Dark: Whiteness in the American Literary Imagination*
Edward Said's *Orientalism*
Gayatri Chakravorty Spivak's *Can the Subaltern Speak?*
Mary Wollstonecraft's *A Vindication of the Rights of Women*
Virginia Woolf's *A Room of One's Own*

PHILOSOPHY

Elizabeth Anscombe's *Modern Moral Philosophy*
Hannah Arendt's *The Human Condition*
Aristotle's *Metaphysics*
Aristotle's *Nicomachean Ethics*
Edmund Gettier's *Is Justified True Belief Knowledge?*
Georg Wilhelm Friedrich Hegel's *Phenomenology of Spirit*
David Hume's *Dialogues Concerning Natural Religion*
David Hume's *The Enquiry for Human Understanding*
Immanuel Kant's *Religion within the Boundaries of Mere Reason*
Immanuel Kant's *Critique of Pure Reason*
Søren Kierkegaard's *The Sickness Unto Death*
Søren Kierkegaard's *Fear and Trembling*
C. S. Lewis's *The Abolition of Man*
Alasdair MacIntyre's *After Virtue*
Marcus Aurelius's *Meditations*
Friedrich Nietzsche's *On the Genealogy of Morality*
Friedrich Nietzsche's *Beyond Good and Evil*
Plato's *Republic*
Plato's *Symposium*
Jean-Jacques Rousseau's *The Social Contract*
Gilbert Ryle's *The Concept of Mind*
Baruch Spinoza's *Ethics*
Sun Tzu's *The Art of War*
Ludwig Wittgenstein's *Philosophical Investigations*

POLITICS

Benedict Anderson's *Imagined Communities*
Aristotle's *Politics*
Bernard Bailyn's *The Ideological Origins of the American Revolution*
Edmund Burke's *Reflections on the Revolution in France*
John C. Calhoun's *A Disquisition on Government*
Ha-Joon Chang's *Kicking Away the Ladder*
Hamid Dabashi's *Iran: A People Interrupted*
Hamid Dabashi's *Theology of Discontent: The Ideological Foundation of the Islamic Revolution in Iran*
Robert Dahl's *Democracy and its Critics*
Robert Dahl's *Who Governs?*
David Brion Davis's *The Problem of Slavery in the Age of Revolution*

Alexis De Tocqueville's *Democracy in America*
James Ferguson's *The Anti-Politics Machine*
Frank Dikotter's *Mao's Great Famine*
Sheila Fitzpatrick's *Everyday Stalinism*
Eric Foner's *Reconstruction: America's Unfinished Revolution, 1863-1877*
Milton Friedman's *Capitalism and Freedom*
Francis Fukuyama's *The End of History and the Last Man*
John Lewis Gaddis's *We Now Know: Rethinking Cold War History*
Ernest Gellner's *Nations and Nationalism*
David Graeber's *Debt: the First 5000 Years*
Antonio Gramsci's *The Prison Notebooks*
Alexander Hamilton, John Jay & James Madison's *The Federalist Papers*
Friedrich Hayek's *The Road to Serfdom*
Christopher Hill's *The World Turned Upside Down*
Thomas Hobbes's *Leviathan*
John A. Hobson's *Imperialism: A Study*
Samuel P. Huntington's *The Clash of Civilizations and the Remaking of World Order*
Tony Judt's *Postwar: A History of Europe Since 1945*
David C. Kang's *China Rising: Peace, Power and Order in East Asia*
Paul Kennedy's *The Rise and Fall of Great Powers*
Robert Keohane's *After Hegemony*
Martin Luther King Jr.'s *Why We Can't Wait*
Henry Kissinger's *World Order: Reflections on the Character of Nations and the Course of History*
John Locke's *Two Treatises of Government*
Niccolò Machiavelli's *The Prince*
Thomas Robert Malthus's *An Essay on the Principle of Population*
Mahmood Mamdani's *Citizen and Subject: Contemporary Africa And The Legacy Of
Late Colonialism*
Karl Marx's *Capital*
John Stuart Mill's *On Liberty*
John Stuart Mill's *Utilitarianism*
Hans Morgenthau's *Politics Among Nations*
Thomas Paine's *Common Sense*
Thomas Paine's *Rights of Man*
Thomas Piketty's *Capital in the Twenty-First Century*
Robert D. Putman's *Bowling Alone*
John Rawls's *Theory of Justice*
Jean-Jacques Rousseau's *The Social Contract*
Theda Skocpol's *States and Social Revolutions*
Adam Smith's *The Wealth of Nations*
Sun Tzu's *The Art of War*
Henry David Thoreau's *Civil Disobedience*
Thucydides's *The History of the Peloponnesian War*
Kenneth Waltz's *Theory of International Politics*
Max Weber's *Politics as a Vocation*
Odd Arne Westad's *The Global Cold War: Third World Interventions And The Making Of Our Times*

POSTCOLONIAL STUDIES

Roland Barthes's *Mythologies*
Frantz Fanon's *Black Skin, White Masks*
Homi K. Bhabha's *The Location of Culture*
Gustavo Gutiérrez's *A Theology of Liberation*
Edward Said's *Orientalism*
Gayatri Chakravorty Spivak's *Can the Subaltern Speak?*

PSYCHOLOGY

Gordon Allport's *The Nature of Prejudice*
Alan Baddeley & Graham Hitch's *Aggression: A Social Learning Analysis*
Albert Bandura's *Aggression: A Social Learning Analysis*
Leon Festinger's *A Theory of Cognitive Dissonance*
Sigmund Freud's *The Interpretation of Dreams*
Betty Friedan's *The Feminine Mystique*
Michael R. Gottfredson & Travis Hirschi's *A General Theory of Crime*
Eric Hoffer's *The True Believer: Thoughts on the Nature of Mass Movements*
William James's *Principles of Psychology*
Elizabeth Loftus's *Eyewitness Testimony*
A. H. Maslow's *A Theory of Human Motivation*
Stanley Milgram's *Obedience to Authority*
Steven Pinker's *The Better Angels of Our Nature*
Oliver Sacks's *The Man Who Mistook His Wife For a Hat*
Richard Thaler & Cass Sunstein's *Nudge: Improving Decisions About Health, Wealth and Happiness*
Amos Tversky's *Judgment under Uncertainty: Heuristics and Biases*
Philip Zimbardo's *The Lucifer Effect*

SCIENCE

Rachel Carson's *Silent Spring*
William Cronon's *Nature's Metropolis: Chicago And The Great West*
Alfred W. Crosby's *The Columbian Exchange*
Charles Darwin's *On the Origin of Species*
Richard Dawkin's *The Selfish Gene*
Thomas Kuhn's *The Structure of Scientific Revolutions*
Geoffrey Parker's *Global Crisis: War, Climate Change and Catastrophe in the Seventeenth Century*
Mathis Wackernagel & William Rees's *Our Ecological Footprint*

SOCIOLOGY

Michelle Alexander's *The New Jim Crow: Mass Incarceration in the Age of Colorblindness*
Gordon Allport's *The Nature of Prejudice*
Albert Bandura's *Aggression: A Social Learning Analysis*
Hanna Batatu's *The Old Social Classes And The Revolutionary Movements Of Iraq*
Ha-Joon Chang's *Kicking Away the Ladder*
W. E. B. Du Bois's *The Souls of Black Folk*
Émile Durkheim's *On Suicide*
Frantz Fanon's *Black Skin, White Masks*
Frantz Fanon's *The Wretched of the Earth*
Eric Foner's *Reconstruction: America's Unfinished Revolution, 1863-1877*
Eugene Genovese's *Roll, Jordan, Roll: The World the Slaves Made*
Jack Goldstone's *Revolution and Rebellion in the Early Modern World*
Antonio Gramsci's *The Prison Notebooks*
Richard Herrnstein & Charles A Murray's *The Bell Curve: Intelligence and Class Structure in American Life*
Eric Hoffer's *The True Believer: Thoughts on the Nature of Mass Movements*
Jane Jacobs's *The Death and Life of Great American Cities*
Robert Lucas's *Why Doesn't Capital Flow from Rich to Poor Countries?*
Jay Macleod's *Ain't No Makin' It: Aspirations and Attainment in a Low Income Neighborhood*
Elaine May's *Homeward Bound: American Families in the Cold War Era*
Douglas McGregor's *The Human Side of Enterprise*
C. Wright Mills's *The Sociological Imagination*

Thomas Piketty's *Capital in the Twenty-First Century*
Robert D. Putman's *Bowling Alone*
David Riesman's *The Lonely Crowd: A Study of the Changing American Character*
Edward Said's *Orientalism*
Joan Wallach Scott's *Gender and the Politics of History*
Theda Skocpol's *States and Social Revolutions*
Max Weber's *The Protestant Ethic and the Spirit of Capitalism*

THEOLOGY

Augustine's *Confessions*
Benedict's *Rule of St Benedict*
Gustavo Gutiérrez's *A Theology of Liberation*
Carole Hillenbrand's *The Crusades: Islamic Perspectives*
David Hume's *Dialogues Concerning Natural Religion*
Immanuel Kant's *Religion within the Boundaries of Mere Reason*
Ernst Kantorowicz's *The King's Two Bodies: A Study in Medieval Political Theology*
Søren Kierkegaard's *The Sickness Unto Death*
C. S. Lewis's *The Abolition of Man*
Saba Mahmood's *The Politics of Piety: The Islamic Revival and the Feminist Subject*
Baruch Spinoza's *Ethics*
Keith Thomas's *Religion and the Decline of Magic*

COMING SOON

Chris Argyris's *The Individual and the Organisation*
Seyla Benhabib's *The Rights of Others*
Walter Benjamin's *The Work Of Art in the Age of Mechanical Reproduction*
John Berger's *Ways of Seeing*
Pierre Bourdieu's *Outline of a Theory of Practice*
Mary Douglas's *Purity and Danger*
Roland Dworkin's *Taking Rights Seriously*
James G. March's *Exploration and Exploitation in Organisational Learning*
Ikujiro Nonaka's *A Dynamic Theory of Organizational Knowledge Creation*
Griselda Pollock's *Vision and Difference*
Amartya Sen's *Inequality Re-Examined*
Susan Sontag's *On Photography*
Yasser Tabbaa's *The Transformation of Islamic Art*
Ludwig von Mises's *Theory of Money and Credit*

The Macat Library By Discipline